# DEFINING MOMENTS
## THE BATTLE OF GETTYSBURG

# DEFINING MOMENTS
# THE BATTLE OF GETTYSBURG

Kevin Hillstrom

*Omnigraphics*

155 W. Congress, Suite 200
Detroit, MI 48226

# Omnigraphics, Inc.

Kevin Hillstrom, *Series Editor*
Cherie D. Abbey, *Managing Editor*

Peter E. Ruffner, *Publisher*
Matthew P. Barbour, *Senior Vice President*

Elizabeth Collins, *Research and Permissions Coordinator*
Kevin M. Hayes, *Operations Manager*

Mary Butler, *Researcher*
Shirley Amore, Joseph Harris, Martha Johns, and Kirk Kauffmann, *Administrative Staff*

**Library of Congress Cataloging-in-Publication Data**

Hillstrom, Kevin, 1963-
    The Battle of Gettysburg / by Kevin Hillstrom.
        pages cm. -- (Defining moments)
    Includes bibliographical references and index.
    Summary: "A detailed account of the American Civil War and the importance of the Battle of Gettysburg. Examines the forces that contributed to the war; early military battles and the Battle of Gettysburg; and the legacy of the Civil War. Also includes biographies, primary sources, chronology, glossary, bibliography, and index"--Provided by publisher.
    ISBN 978-0-7808-1323-6 (hardcover)
    1. Gettysburg, Battle of, Gettysburg, Pa., 1863. I. Title.
    E475.53.H56 2013
    973.7'349--dc23                                                          2012040628

# TABLE OF CONTENTS

## PRIMARY SOURCES

# PREFACE

Throughout the course of America's existence, its people, culture, and institutions have been periodically challenged—and in many cases transformed—by profound historical events. Some of these momentous events, such as women's suffrage, the civil rights movement, and U.S. involvement in World War II, invigorated the nation and strengthened American confidence and capabilities. Others, such as the Great Depression, the Vietnam War, and Watergate, have prompted troubled assessments and heated debates about the country's core beliefs and character.

Some of these defining moments in American history were years or even decades in the making. The Harlem Renaissance and the New Deal, for example, unfurled over the span of several years, while the American labor movement and the Cold War evolved over the course of decades. Other defining moments, such as the Cuban missile crisis and the Japanese attack on Pearl Harbor, transpired over a matter of days or weeks.

But although significant differences exist among these events in terms of their duration and their place in the timeline of American history, all share the same basic characteristic: they transformed the United States' political, cultural, and social landscape for future generations of Americans.

Taking heed of this fundamental reality, American citizens, schools, and other institutions are increasingly emphasizing the importance of understanding our nation's history. Omnigraphics' *Defining Moments* series was created for the express purpose of meeting this growing appetite for authoritative, useful historical resources. This series will be of enduring value to anyone interested in learning more about America's past—and in understanding how those historical events continue to reverberate in the twenty-first century.

Each individual volume of *Defining Moments* provides a valuable resource for readers interested in learning about the most profound events in our nation's history. Each volume is organized into three distinct sections—Narrative Overview, Biographies, and Primary Sources.

- The **Narrative Overview** provides readers with a detailed, factual account of the origins and progression of the "defining moment" being examined. It also explores the event's lasting impact on America's political and cultural landscape.

- The **Biographies** section provides valuable biographical background on leading figures associated with the event in question. Each biography concludes with a list of sources for further information on the profiled individual.

- The **Primary Sources** section collects a wide variety of pertinent primary source materials from the era under discussion, including official documents, papers and resolutions, letters, oral histories, memoirs, editorials, and other important works.

Individually, each of these sections is a rich resource for users. Together, they comprise an authoritative, balanced, and absorbing examination of some of the most significant events in U.S. history.

Other notable features contained within each volume in the series include a glossary of important individuals, places, and terms; a detailed chronology featuring page references to relevant sections of the narrative; an annotated bibliography of sources for further study; an extensive general bibliography that reflects the wide range of historical sources consulted by the author; and a subject index.

## New Feature—Research Topics for Student Reports

Each volume in the *Defining Moments* series now includes a list of potential research topics for students. Students working on historical research and writing assignments will find this feature especially useful in assessing their options.

Information on the highlighted research topics can be found throughout the different sections of the book—and especially in the narrative overview, biography, and primary source sections. This wide coverage gives readers the flexibility to study the topic through multiple entry points.

## Acknowledgements

This series was developed in consultation with a distinguished Advisory Board comprised of public librarians, school librarians, and educators. They evaluated the series as it developed, and their comments and suggestions were invaluable throughout the production process. Any errors in this and other volumes in the series are ours alone. Following is a list of board members who contributed to the *Defining Moments* series:

## Comments and Suggestions

We welcome your comments on *Defining Moments: The Battle of Gettysburg* and suggestions for other events in U.S. history that warrant treatment in the *Defining Moments* series. Correspondence should be addressed to:

Editor, *Defining Moments*
Omnigraphics, Inc.
155 West Congress, Suite 200
Detroit, MI 48226
E-mail: editorial@omnigraphics.com

# HOW TO USE THIS BOOK

D*efining Moments: The Battle of Gettysburg* provides users with a detailed and authoritative overview of this pivotal episode in U.S. history. The preparation and arrangement of this volume—and all other books in the *Defining Moments* series—reflect an emphasis on providing a thorough and objective account of events that shaped our nation, presented in an easy-to-use reference work.

*The Battle of Gettysburg* is divided into three main sections. The first of these sections, **Narrative Overview**, provides a detailed account of the American Civil War and the importance of the Battle of Gettysburg in shaping the outcome of that conflict. The section opens by explaining how the practice of slavery in the South and the growth of the abolitionist movement in the North created deep political, cultural, and economic ruptures in the United States. It then delves into the Civil War itself, guiding readers through the various military battles and maneuverings that led to the showdown at Gettysburg. The overview also provides in-depth coverage of all three days of the Battle of Gettysburg, including the famous Day Three assault popularly known as "Pickett's Charge," and Abraham Lincoln's famous Gettysburg Address. It concludes with an examination of the legacy of the Civil War (and its most famous battle) on American history and culture.

The second section, **Biographies**, provides informative biographical profiles of Union and Confederate military and political leaders who played prominent roles at Gettysburg. Featured individuals from the ranks of the Confederacy include Robert E. Lee, James Longstreet, George Pickett, and J. E. B. Stuart. Union military commanders such as George G. Meade, John Buford, Winfield Hancock, and Joshua Lawrence Chamberlain are also profiled, as is President Abraham Lincoln.

The third section, **Primary Sources**, collects essential and illuminating documents on the Battle of Gettysburg and the wider Civil War. Featured primary sources in this volume include firsthand accounts of the bloodshed at Gettysburg from Robert E. Lee, George Meade, Joshua Lawrence Chamberlain, James Longstreet, and other military commanders; remembrances of Pickett's Charge from infantry soldiers wearing both blue and gray; Lincoln's historic Gettysburg Address; and President Woodrow Wilson's remarks at the reunion of Gettysburg veterans held on the fiftieth anniversary of the famous battle.

Other valuable features in *Defining Moments: The Battle of Gettysburg* include the following:

- Attribution and referencing of primary sources and other quoted material to help guide users to other valuable historical research resources.
- Glossary of Important People, Places, and Terms.
- Detailed Chronology of events with a *see reference* feature. Under this arrangement, events listed in the chronology include a reference to page numbers within the Narrative Overview wherein users can find additional information on the event in question.
- Photographs of the leading figures and major events associated with the American Civil War and the Battle of Gettysburg.
- Sources for Further Study, an annotated list of noteworthy works about the Battle of Gettysburg and the Civil War.
- Extensive bibliography of works consulted in the creation of this book, including books, periodicals, and Internet sites.
- A Subject Index.

# RESEARCH TOPICS FOR
## DEFINING MOMENTS:
## THE BATTLE OF GETTYSBURG

When students receive an assignment to produce a research paper on a historical event or topic, the first step in that process—settling on a subject for the paper—can also be one of the most vexing. In recognition of that reality, each book in the *Defining Moments* series now highlights research areas/topics that receive extensive coverage within that particular volume.

Potential research topics for students using *Defining Moments: The Battle of Gettysburg* include the following:

- Explain the central role that slavery played in the rising tensions between America's northern and southern states, and the South's efforts to portray its stance on slavery as an issue of "states' rights."

- List reasons why the election of Abraham Lincoln to the presidency of the United States in 1860 convinced slaveholding states to secede.

- Provide reasons why both the North and South believed that the Civil War would end quickly—and why each side was certain that it would be victorious.

- Discuss the main military problems that afflicted the Union and Confederate armies during the first two years of the war.

- Explain the importance of having possession of high ground in military battles such as the one that took place at Gettysburg in July 1863.

- Compare and contrast the performance of the two armies during the first two days at Gettysburg, paying particular attention to the orders of top commanders like Lee, Longstreet, Hill, Ewell, Grant, Meade, Hancock, and Sickles.

- Compare and contrast the Confederate assaults at Chancellorsville and at Gettysburg on Day Three a mere two months later. What factors contributed to the success of the first charge and the failure of the second?
- Why does Lincoln's Gettysburg Address continue to have such a prominent place in American history and culture?
- The Battle of Gettysburg and the Civil War hold a prominent place in the minds of Americans. Discuss the legacy of these events on American history and culture.

# NARRATIVE OVERVIEW

# PROLOGUE

For two and a half days the battle had raged outside the little southern Pennsylvania town of Gettysburg, leaving the corpses of soldiers and horses strewn all across the surrounding countryside. During that time the army clad in gray—Robert E. Lee's Army of Northern Virginia, the pride and joy of the Confederacy—had repeatedly pummeled the defenses of the blue-clad warriors—George Meade's Army of the Potomac, the largest of the armies that comprised the Union's military machine. On each occasion, though, Lee's divisions had been turned back after hours of vicious struggle. The offensives soaked the ground of once-pastoral tracts of farmland with Yankee and Rebel blood, but they failed to dislodge Meade's forces from the high, wooded ridges and hills that marked the southern ramparts of the now-abandoned town.

The desperate combat waged by the opposing armies reflected a keen understanding of the stakes involved. Lee had been pummeling and embarrassing Union armies for two years, and he had come to believe that a decisive victory over the Army of the Potomac—on Northern territory, no less—might finally convince President Abraham Lincoln and his fellow Northerners to admit defeat and let the Confederate States of America go their separate way. Meade and his generals, on the other hand, recognized that a Union victory at Gettysburg would finally pierce the aura of invincibility that surrounded Lee and the Army of Northern Virginia. Such a blow might not only cripple the Confederate army, but also revitalize the spirits of despondent lawmakers, soldiers, and civilians all across the North.

When the Confederate artillery opened up on the center of the Union defenses at Cemetery Ridge midway through the third day of battle—July 3, 1863—Meade and his top officers sensed that one more mighty Rebel offensive was approaching. This belief hardened into certainty as the barrage pounded Cemetery Ridge for two solid hours in a clear attempt to soften up the Union defenses for another infantry assault. The Federal troops in blue answered with their own deadly rain of shells. The smoke, roar, and devastation of these twin bombardments led Lieutenant Frank A. Haskell of the Army of the Potomac's Second Corps, which was stationed at the heart of Cemetery Ridge, to compare the battleground to the pits of Hades. "To say that it was like a summer storm, with the crash of thunder, the glare of lightning, the shrieking of the wind, and the clatter of hailstones, would be weak," Haskell wrote. "The thunder and lightning of these 250 guns and their shells, whose smoke darkens the sky, are incessant, all pervading, in the air above our heads, on the ground at our feet, remote, near, deafening, ear-piercing, astounding; and these hailstones are massy iron, charged with exploding fire."[1]

At 3:00 p.m. the guns finally fell silent. But the quiet that descended over Gettysburg was not a peaceful one. The Union troops standing behind the stone walls that ran along the crest of Cemetery Ridge knew that the Rebel artillery barrage was only a prelude to the main event. They waited tensely as the minutes ticked by, checking their rifles and ammunition, whispering quiet prayers, and rifling through their pockets to look at pictures of their loved ones, possibly for the last time. And at 4:00 p.m. their wait came to an end, as Haskell recalled years later:

> We met Captain Wessels and the orderlies who had our horses; they were on foot leading the horses. Captain [Francis] Wessels was pale, and he said, excited: "General [John Gibbon], they say the enemy's infantry is advancing." We sprang into our saddles, [and] a score of bounds brought us upon the all-seeing crest. To say that men grew pale and held their breath at what we and they there saw, would not be true. Might not 6,000 men be brave and without shade of fear, and yet, before a hostile 18,000, armed, and not five minutes' march away, turn ashy white? None on that crest now need be told that *the enemy is advancing*. Every eye could see the enemy's legions, an overwhelming resistless tide of an ocean of armed men sweeping upon us! Regiment after regiment and brigade after brigade move from the woods and rapidly take their places in the line forming the assault. [Confederate general George] Pickett's proud division with some additional troops hold their right. The first line at short intervals is followed by a second, and that a third succeeds; and columns between support the lines. More than half a mile their

front extends; more than a thousand yards the dull gray mass-es deploy, man touching man, rank pressing rank and line sup-porting line. The red flags wave, their horsemen gallop up and down; the arms of 18,000 men, barrel and bayonet, gleam in the sun, a sloping forest of flashing steel. Right on they move, as with one soul, in perfect order, without impediment of ditch or wall or stream, over ridge and slope, through orchard and mead-ow and cornfield, magnificent, grim, irresistible.[2]

This great assault—known forever after as Pickett's Charge—would decide the Battle of Gettysburg once and for all. And in the process, say Civil War his-torians, it would change the course of American history.

## Notes

[1] Haskell, Frank Aretas. *The Battle of Gettysburg*. 1898. Boston: Commandery of the State of Massa-chusetts, Military Order of the Loyal Legion, 1908, p. 50.
[2] Haskell, p. 58.

# Chapter One

# SLAVERY THREATENS
# THE UNION

So I say in relation to the principle that all men are created equal,
let it be as nearly reached as we can.... I leave you, hoping that
the lamp of liberty will burn in your bosoms until there shall no
longer be a doubt that all men are created free and equal.

—Abraham Lincoln, 1858

Slavery was a prominent feature of the British colonies that took root along the Atlantic seaboard of North America in the seventeenth and eighteenth centuries. Early English settlers used African slaves to help them clear land, build homes and barns, plant and harvest crops, and tend livestock. Most of the British colonists were pretty comfortable with the idea of enslaving African men, women, and children. They persuaded themselves that the "savages" and "primitives" who had been forcibly removed from their homes in Africa were actually better off in America, where their white owners could teach them Christianity and provide them with life's basic necessities.

As the 1700s unfolded, though, some religious groups began describing slavery as an evil practice that should be abolished throughout the colonies. The most vocal of these groups was the Society of Friends, better known as the Quakers. Victims of religious persecution in England, the Quakers played a leading role in the settlement of both Pennsylvania and New Jersey. By the 1750s, Quaker religious leaders were describing slavery as a source of moral shame in the colonies. "To live in ease and plenty, by the toil of those, whom violence and cruelty have put in our power, is neither consistent with Christianity nor common justice,"[1] said Philadelphia Quaker Anthony Benezet in 1754. Twenty-one years later, Benezet would help co-found America's first anti-slavery society, the Pennsylvania Abolition Society, with Benjamin Franklin and Thomas Paine.

## A Constitutional Compromise on Slavery

During the 1770s and early 1780s the debate over slavery was eclipsed by the Revolutionary War, which pitted rebellious colonists against British troops and settlers loyal to the English crown. After the rebels gained their independence and formed the United States of America in 1783, however, the issue of slavery returned with a vengeance. America's so-called Founding Fathers—the generals, statesmen, and writers who had led the long and arduous fight for independence from England—wanted freedom, liberty, and democracy to be the central pillars of the new nation they were building. To continue allowing slavery in such a world struck many of America's early leaders as the height of hypocrisy. These emerging views led Northern states to begin passing laws that outlawed involvement in the slave trade and provided for the gradual emancipation of Africans in bondage.

> *"We have the wolf [of slavery] by the ear, and we can neither hold him, nor safely let him go. Justice is in one scale, and self-preservation in the other."*
> *– Thomas Jefferson*

Yet the young nation was intensely vulnerable in its early days of existence. Many Americans worried that if an attempt was made to abolish slavery immediately, Southern states that remained heavily dependent on slavery for agricultural labor would refuse to join the new nation. The United States might fall apart before it ever got a chance to establish itself.

These fears about slavery's explosive potential led America's early leaders to opt for stability over idealism when they gathered in Philadelphia in the summer of 1787 for the Constitutional Convention. Over the course of four months, these delegates from the former British colonies produced the U.S. Constitution, which became the nation's legal and political foundation when it was ratified in 1788. The Constitution is widely lauded today for its eloquence, wisdom, and enduring power. Nonetheless, its creators avoided taking a firm stance on slavery. In fact, the words "slave" and slavery" do not even appear in the document. Instead, the creators of the Constitution used euphemisms—code words—for slavery, which they handled through a series of tensely negotiated compromises.

The most famous Constitutional clause regarding the "peculiar institution," as slavery was sometimes called, counted each slave as three-fifths of a

George Washington presiding over the Constitutional Convention in Philadelphia, during which the Founding Fathers agreed to count slaves as three-fifths of a person for purposes of Congressional representation.

man in the U.S. Census for purposes of congressional representation. This was a big win for Southern slaveholding states, because each state's representation in the U.S. Congress—and thus its political influence—depended on the size of its population. In addition, pro-slavery delegates to the Constitutional Convention managed to insert a fugitive slave clause to help slaveholders regain possession of runaway slaves living in the North.

In return, Southern delegates agreed to keep the Northwest Territory—a huge section of land acquired from Great Britain in 1783—free of slavery. This was an important concession, since the region encompassed all of five future states (Illinois, Indiana, Michigan, Ohio, and Wisconsin) and part of another (Minnesota). In addition, the Constitution included a clause that ended U.S. imports of slaves from overseas—but only after a twenty-year grace period that was insisted on by the Georgia and South Carolina delegations.

Some historians have said that these compromises might have been the best deal that abolitionists could have achieved at the time. They also point out that many Northerners believed that universal emancipation was just a matter of time—but that it needed to be carried out slowly and carefully to minimize social, economic, and political unrest. This sentiment was clearly expressed by Oliver Ellsworth, one of the signers of the Constitution, a few months after the Convention adjourned: "All good men wish the entire abolition of slavery, as soon as it can take place with safety to the public, and for the lasting good of the present wretched race of slaves."[2] A similar view was offered in 1786 by George Washington, who called for "slavery in this country [to be] abolished by slow, sure, & imperceptable degrees."[3]

Some historians, however, believe that all of these excuses do not obscure the fact that the delegates failed to live up to the Constitution's stated belief that "all men are created equal." "Their concern for harmony within the Convention was much stronger than their concern for the fate of those Africans whose lives and labor would be sacrificed by the continuation of the slave trade," wrote constitutional scholar Richard Beeman. "The delegates made a fugitive-slave clause an integral part of our federal compact. It was the one act of the Convention that not only signaled the delegates' grudging acceptance of slavery but also made the states that had moved either to abolish or gradually eliminate slavery in the aftermath of the Revolution actively complicit in their support of that institution."[4]

## Distinct Economies and Cultures

Abolitionist hopes that slavery in America would die a natural death were dashed in the final years of the eighteenth century by a revolutionary new invention called the cotton gin. This simple but ingenious machine was unveiled by Massachusetts native Eli Whitney in 1793. The cotton gin quickly and effectively separated cotton seeds from the white fiber used to make clothing, blankets, and other goods. The device transformed agriculture in the South, which possessed soil and weather that was ideal for cotton production. Small farmers and wealthy planters alike began devoting most of their fields to "King Cotton," which commanded high prices from manufacturers based in the North and in Europe.

The surge in cotton production, though, also made the South much more dependent on slavery for its economic health and vitality. For although the cotton gin cleaned the crop for sale, plantation owners still needed large numbers of laborers to *pick* the cotton. As the amount of land set aside for cotton soared, so too did the demand for slaves. In 1808 the U.S. Congress formally banned the importation of slaves onto American soil, but the law did not reduce the South's heavy dependence on slaves. Instead, Southern planters used black market shipments of slaves and the children of existing slaves to replenish their labor force. By 1860 there were nearly four million slaves toiling in America's slave states.

At the same time that the South was tying its economic fortunes to slavery, the North charted a much different path. The cities of the North embraced new machines, technologies, and manufacturing processes that came to be collectively known as the "Industrial Revolution." The factories that were created through these processes depended on natural resources like coal, iron, and timber that the North possessed in abundance. The Northern states also invested heavily in railroads, canals, harbors, and roads. This transportation network not only made it easier for Northerners to deliver coal, cotton, and other raw materials to their hungry factories, it also enabled manufacturers to sell their prod-

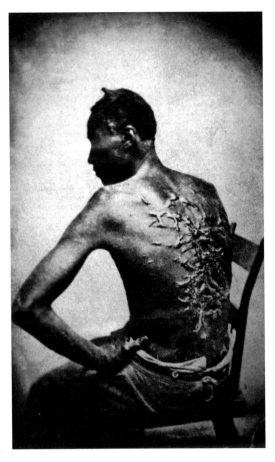

The back of this Louisiana slave provides grim evidence that Southern slave owners had complete freedom to whip or otherwise assault their "property" whenever they wished.

ucts to customers who lived and worked several states away. These roaring factories and shipyards never became dependent on slave labor, though. Instead, they were manned by a mix of native-born white Americans, free blacks, and European immigrants who worked long hours in dangerous jobs for meager pay.

## Territorial Expansion Increases Tensions

As the economy of the South became ever more slave-dependent, the waves of disapproval from the slave-free states of the North increased in intensity.

Former President Thomas Jefferson predicted that the Missouri Compromise was doomed to fail.

These tensions deepened with America's rapid territorial expansion. From 1803 to 1853, the United States gobbled up land in the West and South in a series of enormous gulps. These acquisitions included the Louisiana Purchase of 1803, the purchase of Florida from Spain in 1819, the addition of the Oregon Territory from England in 1846, the seizure of western lands from Mexico in 1848 at the conclusion of the Mexican-American War, and the Gadsden Purchase of western territory from Mexico in 1853.

Ownership of these new lands greatly excited Americans and European immigrants who were eager to carve better lives for themselves out of the vast tracts of wilderness to the west. This geographic expansion posed big headaches, however, for politicians in Washington. Both slave states and "free" states (ones that outlawed slavery) refused to consider any political arrangements that would place them at a disadvantage in Congress.

When the territory of Missouri petitioned Congress for statehood in 1818, for example, abolitionists in the North objected to Missouri's bid because it wanted to join as a slaveholding state. If Missouri's request was granted, the slave states would get a 12-11 edge over the free states in the union—which would in turn mean that the slaveholding South would gain a two-seat edge in the U.S. Senate over the North (each state is represented by two U.S. senators in Washington). As a result, the antislavery states blocked Missouri's request for statehood for more than a year. This caused a great deal of frustration not only in Missouri, but among Southerners who argued that each state ought to be able to decide for itself whether to allow slavery.

The deadlock was finally broken by Senator Henry Clay of Kentucky. Clay brokered an agreement in which Missouri would be admitted as a slave state—and, at the same time, a new free state called Maine would be formed from land in northern Massachusetts. This so-called Missouri Compromise preserved the balance of power in Congress between slaveholding and free states. In addition, the Missouri Compromise laid down guidelines on how to handle the slavery question when other western territories inevitably requested admittance to the union. The legislation drew a line through the rest of the lands acquired via the Louisiana Purchase at the 36° 30′ latitude line. It stipulated that slavery would only be allowed in states that were created south of that line.

Some Americans hoped that the creation of a slavery boundary line through the midsection of the continent would reduce North-South tensions over slavery. Other men, like Thomas Jefferson, composer of the Declaration of Independence and the nation's third president, were much more skeptical. Jefferson saw the Compromise's formal division of the country into slaveholding and free sections as nothing more than a temporary "reprieve" that would ultimately worsen tensions over slavery. "As it is," he wrote in 1820, "we have the wolf [of slavery] by the ear, and we can neither hold him, nor safely let him go. Justice is in one scale, and self-preservation in the other."[5]

## Abolitionist Voices Grow Louder

In the 1830s and 1840s the abolitionist cause steadily gained new disciples in the North. This growth was due in great measure to the eloquence and persistence of abolitionists like William Lloyd Garrison, Frederick Douglass, Lydia Maria Child, Theodore Weld, and Angelina and Sarah Grimké. Some white abolitionists even joined with free blacks in establishing secret networks to help runaway slaves gain their freedom in the Northern states or Canada. These networks came to be known collectively as the Underground Railroad.

Abolitionist calls for the immediate emancipation of all slaves, and their descriptions of slavery as depraved and un-Christian, infuriated white Southerners. They accurately saw the anti-slavery crusade as an attack on both the morality of the slaveholding South and its economic and cultural foundations. In addition, white Southerners worried that the growing abolitionist talk would encourage slaves to take up arms against their masters—an ever-present fear in the South.

Even poor white Southerners who could not afford slaves chafed at the criticisms coming from the North. Unlike wealthy plantation owners who stood to lose financially from an end to slavery, however, the anger of poor whites was heavily influenced by issues of self-esteem and self-image. No matter how mis-

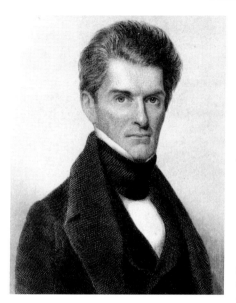

South Carolina senator John C. Calhoun was one of many Southern senators who warned that abolitionism could lead to secession from the Union.

erable or difficult their lives were, the continued existence of slavery ensured that there would always be millions of blacks in the South who were even worse off. This consideration, combined with deep-seated racist beliefs, led poor whites in Mississippi, Kentucky, Virginia, South Carolina, and other Southern states to join the region's white aristocracy in embracing "states' rights"—the idea that the federal government should never possess the power to tell individual states what to do about slavery or any other issue.

During the 1830s and 1840s hostility to abolitionism in the South hardened so much that several state legislatures passed laws outlawing anti-slavery publications or speeches. Whites who had once expressed their own misgivings about slavery fell silent, their voices stilled by accounts of whites who had been terrorized or murdered for speaking out against the institution. Instead, most Southern whites counterattacked against the abolitionists by framing slavery as a moral *benefit* to mankind. "I hold that in the present state of civilization, the relation now existing in the slave-holding states between the two [races] is, instead of an evil, a good—a *positive* good," declared South Carolina senator John C. Calhoun in 1837. Calhoun also warned that if the North did not stop agitating against slavery with such "deadly hatred," the United States would inevitably become "two people.... Abolition and the Union cannot coexist."[6]

Northern supporters of emancipation, meanwhile, continued to deplore slavery as a betrayal of American ideals and the Christian faith. Yet their feelings about black and white equality were complicated and inconsistent. In the 1850s, for instance, many members of the new Republican Party staked out positions in opposition to slavery. But historian Eric Foner pointed out that for every "Radical Republican" like Charles Sumner who "insisted that free blacks ought to enjoy precisely the same rights as white Americans,"[7] there were many Republicans who were not sure just how many civil, social, and political rights African Americans ought to have. Other Republican lawmakers, like Senator

## The Underground Railroad

The Underground Railroad was the symbolic term used to describe a secret system of people and places who helped fugitive slaves escape from the South to freedom in Northern states or Canada. The Railroad was particularly active in the so-called border states directly above the slave-holding South, and especially in the Ohio River Valley.

The individual routes of the Underground Railroad network were operated independently, without oversight or direction from any single organization or person. The routes were maintained primarily by free blacks, but white abolitionists played an important role in many of them as well. In describing their operations, these men and women borrowed heavily from the terminology of the railroads that sprouted across America during the first half of the nineteenth century. They referred to the homes, farms, and businesses where fugitives hid as "stations" or "depots." The men and women who harbored fugitives and helped them move northward to the next hiding place on their route were known as "stationmasters" and "conductors," respectively.

No one knows exactly how many fugitive slaves gained their freedom through the Underground Railroad, but historians estimate that several hundred slaves completed the journey on an annual basis during the 1830s and 1840s. Many conductors and stationmasters provided heroic service during these years, but the most famous of these individuals was probably Harriet Tubman. An escaped slave herself, Tubman made numerous perilous trips back into the slaveholding South in order to guide an estimated 300 slaves to freedom.

Lyman Trumbull of Illinois, expressed less concern with emancipating existing slaves in the South than with keeping the western territories free of slaves in the future. "We are for the free white man," said Trumbull, "and for making white labor acceptable and honorable, which it can never be when negro slave labor is brought into competition with it."[8]

## The Compromise of 1850

In 1848 the tensions over slavery escalated to a fever pitch with the February 1848 signing of the Treaty of Guadalupe Hidalgo, which ended the Mex-

Kentucky senator Henry Clay brokered the Compromise of 1850.

ican-American War. Millions of Americans celebrated the treaty, which forced Mexico to hand over possession of all its northern territories—roughly half of the entire country—to the United States in exchange for a small financial package of $21.5 million. This 525,000-square-mile swath of the West would eventually be converted into all or most of the present-day U.S. states of Arizona, California, Colorado, Nevada, New Mexico, Texas, and Utah, as well as parts of Oklahoma, Kansas, and Wyoming.

The acquisition of this territory was widely hailed as a realization of America's "Manifest Destiny"—the popular belief that Almighty God wanted the United States to spread across the North American continent, tame its reaches of wilderness, and rise above all other nations and peoples. However, the absorption of this new land also resurrected the old problem of maintaining the fragile balance between slave and free states. And by the late 1840s, more and more Northern abolitionists had decided that they could no longer accept that balance; in addition to their calls for emancipation in the South, they insisted that all new states formed out of the frontier West be free states. Southerners responded to this unyielding stance with grim warnings that outlawing slavery in the West might force slave states to secede from the Union entirely.

The issue came to a head in September 1849. Lawmakers in the territory of California, which had experienced a huge surge in population after the discovery of gold in several of its rivers, formally petitioned the U.S. Congress for admittance to the Union as a free state. The South furiously objected, pointing out that such a move—which meant California would gain two U.S. senators—would give free states a stronger voice than slave states in the U.S. Senate.

As both sides hurled insults and threats at one another, Senator Clay once again swooped in to broker a compromise. North and South reluctantly agreed to the so-called Compromise of 1850, although only after a lot of grumbling and expressions of skepticism about its long-term workability. The Compromise actually consisted of five bills that were passed together in September, four of which directly related to slavery. Two of the provisions were favored by the abolitionists. One put an end to the slave trade in the nation's capital, which had for many years been home to one of the country's largest slave markets. The other admitted California into the Union as a free state.

The pro-slavery South accepted these provisions because of two other bills included in the Compromise. The first established that residents of territories in Arizona, New Mexico, Nevada, and Utah could decide for themselves about slavery when they later applied for statehood. This measure weakened the slave boundaries that had been set by the Missouri Compromise back in 1820. The big prize for pro-slavery lawmakers, though, was the Fugitive Slave Act. This law required white citizens anywhere in the country to help slave hunters capture runaway slaves, and it established harsh penalties (including jail terms) for those who failed to do so. It also ordered federal agents to assist in capturing fugitive slaves and stripped accused runaways of their right to a jury trial—or even to testify in their own defense. As a result, blacks who were legally free or who had escaped to the North decades earlier were sometimes arrested and shipped south to spend the rest of their lives in bondage. "The fugitive slave law of 1850 put the burden of proof on captured blacks but gave them no legal power to prove their freedom," wrote historian James M. McPherson. "Instead, a claimant could bring an alleged fugitive before a federal commissioner to prove ownership by an affidavit [sworn statement] from a slave-state court or by the testimony of white witnesses. If the commissioner decided against the claimant he would receive a fee of five dollars; if in favor, ten dollars. This provision, supposedly justified by the paper work needed to remand a fugitive to the South, became notorious among abolitionists as a bribe to commissioners."[9]

## The Kansas-Nebraska Act

The South hailed the passage of the Fugitive Slave Act as a great victory. As time passed, however, it became clear that the law had the unintended consequence of further intensifying Northern antislavery feelings. As Northern newspapers filled up with heart-wrenching stories of slave hunters who used the act to drag hardworking husbands, wives, and parents back to the South, the abolitionist movement gained thousands of new supporters.

Condemnation of slavery soared to even higher levels in 1852, when Harriet Beecher Stowe published her landmark novel *Uncle Tom's Cabin*. Stowe's story swirled around several sympathetic black slaves, including the dignified

Harriett Beecher Stowe's novel *Uncle Tom's Cabin* (1852) became a formidable weapon in the hands of the abolitionist movement.

and self-sacrificing Uncle Tom and a brave and loving mother named Eliza, and a cruel slave owner named Simon Legree. The novel, which Stowe was inspired to write in direct response to the Fugitive Slave Act, provided a tremendous boost to the abolitionist cause. It sold half a million copies in America and England within a year of its publication, and theatrical productions of the story drew immense crowds. Southerners were astonished by the book's impact. They complained that Stowe's book was a malicious fantasy that failed to show the "good" side of slavery.

Emotions over slavery had thus reached a fever pitch in 1854, when Democratic senator Stephen A. Douglas of Illinois crafted and engineered the passage of a law—the Kansas-Nebraska Act—that elicited fresh roars of anger and dismay from abolitionists. The main purpose of Douglas's bill was to establish the route for a proposed transcontinental railroad through Illinois. Such a route would not only bolster Douglas's political popularity but personally enrich him, since he had significant real estate holdings along the proposed route. To secure Southern votes for his proposal, though, Douglas included a provision that effectively gutted the Missouri Compromise of 1820. This was the law that had outlawed slavery in all Western territory above the 36° 30´ latitude line. Under the terms of the Kansas-Nebraska Act, the citizens of the new territories of Kansas and Nebraska would now decide for themselves whether to allow slavery within their borders. "If the people of Kansas want a slaveholding state, let them have it," said Douglas. "And if they want a free state they have a right to it, and it is not for the people of Illinois, or Missouri, or New York, or Kentucky, to complain, whatever the decision of the people of Kansas may be upon that point."[10]

Douglas's justification for the law did not comfort people in the North. Instead, Northern newspapers, legislators, abolitionist activists, and ordinary citizens all interpreted the law as a gateway for slavery to spread all across the

West. One group of anti-slavery con-gressmen from Ohio condemned the bill as the latest chapter in an "atrocious plot [to make the West] a dreary region of despotism, inhabited by masters and slaves.... Whatever apologies may be offered for the toleration of slavery in the States, none can be offered for its exten-sion into Territories where it does not exist." The signers also urged their fellow citizens to resist "this enormous crime ... by speech and vote, and with all the abil-ities which God has given us."[11]

## Bleeding Kansas

Americans on both sides of the slav-ery issue recognized that Nebraska's set-tlers were strongly in the anti-slavery camp, so the people of that territory moved toward statehood with relatively little controversy. The neighboring Kansas territory, however, was up for grabs, so abolitionist and pro-slavery forces poured into Kansas in hopes of swaying the upcoming vote in their

Abolitionist John Brown responded to the attack on Lawrence, Kansas, by pro-slavery guerrillas with a killing spree that took the lives of five white pro-slavery settlers.

favor. Both sides were convinced that the Kansas outcome would ultimately determine whether slavery would spread throughout much of the West.

The next two years brought a frenzy of political maneuvering and violence across Kansas. By mid-1856 the territory even had two legislatures, one that championed slavery and another devoted to making it an anti-slavery "free soil" state. Some members of the latter camp, however, did not really care about the welfare of African Americans. They wanted to keep slavery out because they believed it would make it easier for white settlers to acquire land.

As these two legislative bodies jockeyed for advantage, violence between supporters and opponents of slavery steadily escalated across the territory, which came to be known as "Bleeding Kansas." In one famous incident, a mob of pro-slavery "ruffians" from Missouri rode into the abolitionist town of Lawrence on May 21, 1856, and ransacked the place. Abolitionist John Brown and several followers responded to this terrorist act by kidnapping five pro-slavery settlers and hacking them to death with swords.

The violence in Kansas did not begin to subside until late 1856, when new territorial governor John White Geary made effective use of federal troops to stem the tide of outside agitators and establish a measure of stability for law-abiding Kansans. In mid-1859 "free soil" forces passed a constitution that could be used in petitioning the U.S. Congress for statehood. Bitter senators from the slave states managed to bottle up Kansas's application for statehood for the next two years, but when the Southern states seceded from the Union in 1861 the constitution was approved and Kansas became America's thirty-fourth state.

## Democrats and Republicans React to *Dred Scott*

The Kansas-Nebraska Act also set off a chain of events that ushered in a new age of American politics. The Whig Party, which had been established in the 1830s, had come under great strain because of internal divisions over the slavery issue. After the Kansas-Nebraska Act, the party finally buckled altogether. Southern Whigs fled to the pro-slavery Democratic Party, and Northern Whigs joined forces with "free soil" advocates to create an anti-slavery Republican Party concentrated in the North.

During the 1850s, the Democrats carved out a commanding position in the South. They became weaker in the North, however, as antislavery sentiment increased and the Republican brand became more familiar to voters. Republican unity in the North became particularly strong in the aftermath of an 1857 ruling by the U.S. Supreme Court that, more than a century and a half later, remains one of the most notorious and heavily criticized Court decisions in American history.

The infamous *Dred Scott v. Sandford* case focused on whether a Missouri slave named Dred Scott should be granted his freedom after spending many years with his master (since deceased) in states and territories that did not allow slavery. Scott's appeal was turned down by a 7-2 vote, with Chief Justice Roger Taney and four other justices from slaveholding states in the majority.

The reasoning behind this judgment triggered a firestorm of fury in the North. Taney and his allies on the Court said that Scott did not have the right to bring the case before the Court in the first place because he was not a U.S. citizen. The majority then went on to declare that according to their interpretation of the Constitution, *no* blacks—even free blacks and their descendants—

could ever become citizens of the United States. Blacks were thus forever blocked from voting or from exercising basic legal rights available to white Americans. The Founding Fathers, wrote Taney, believed that blacks "had no rights which a white man was bound to respect."

Taney and the other members of the *Dred Scott* majority also opened the doorway for slavery in the Western territories. They struck down the Missouri Compromise as unconstitutional and declared that the federal government had no legal right to outlaw slavery anywhere in the West since slaves were the "private property" of their white owners.

The announcement of this decision on March 6, 1857, triggered dramatically different responses from the two parties. Democratic lawmakers and newspaper publishers rejoiced. Democratic President James Buchanan stated in early 1858 that slavery now was legal in Kansas

In 1857 the U.S. Supreme Court forced a former slave named Dred Scott back into bondage, further deepening North-South tensions over slavery.

and the rest of the territories "by virtue of the Constitution."[12] Republicans congressmen and newspapers in the North were enraged. Many state legislatures passed resolutions to formally give blacks citizenship in their states, and Maine's legislators approved a resolution that flatly refused to recognize the legitimacy of the *Dred Scott* decision. The *Cleveland Leader* spoke for most Republicans when it summarized Taney's ruling as "villainously false."[13]

## The 1860 Presidential Campaign

By the time the 1860 presidential campaign came into view, the upheaval over the Fugitive Slave Act, *Uncle Tom's Cabin*, the Kansas-Nebraska Act, *Dred Scott*, and "Bloody Kansas" had enveloped the United States in a fog of fear, anger, and suspicion. As historian Bruce Catton wrote, slavery had become "the issue that could not be compromised, the issue that made men so angry they did not want to compromise."[14]

Both the Republican and Democratic parties recognized that the winner of the 1860 election would strongly influence the future of slavery in Ameri-

A campaign banner for the 1860 Republican ticket featuring presidential nominee Abraham Lincoln and vice presidential nominee Hannibal Hamlin.

ca. In fairly short order the Republicans chose a moderate antislavery politician from Illinois named Abraham Lincoln as their candidate (see Lincoln biography, p. 143). The Democratic Party, however, became tangled in a nasty power struggle between its Northern and Southern wings over the best nominee (Buchanan could have run for re-election, but he had promised to only serve one term—and by 1860 he was widely unpopular).

The Democratic Party split apart at its nominating convention in June 1860. A large band of Southern delegates known as "fire-eaters"—radical supporters of slavery who spoke openly of secession from the United States—walked out of the convention. They refused to support the favored candidate of the Northern wing, Illinois senator Stephen Douglas, despite the fact that he had defeated Lincoln two years earlier in a heavily publicized U.S. Senate race. The fire-eaters did not trust Douglas to defend slavery with sufficient vigor, so they nominated their own candidate, John C. Breckinridge. A native of Kentucky who held strong pro-slavery views, Breckinridge was the incumbent vice

On April 12, 1861, however, events in South Carolina dramatically changed the complexion of the tense standoff between Lincoln and the secessionists. That evening, South Carolina militia attacked Fort Sumter, which was located on an island in South Carolina's Charleston Harbor. Fort Sumter was one of only four military outposts that had remained under Union control after the formation of the Confederacy (the other three were along the lightly populated Florida coastline). The station was lightly defended and cut off from much-needed supplies, so the bombardment from Confederate guns left the fort's garrison with little choice but to surrender the next day.

News of the violence at Fort Sumter resounded across both North and South like a great thunderbolt. It convinced Lincoln and his closest advisors that the administration would have to restore the Union by force. To that end, Lincoln issued two proclamations in mid-April calling for Union states to recruit a total of 150,000 soldiers for national service for ninety days. The states had no trouble finding volunteers, for the attack on Fort Sumter had outraged people all across the North. They knew that full-fledged war was on the horizon, and they were eager to defend the Union's honor.

*In his inaugural address in 1860, President Lincoln described Southern secession as "the essence of anarchy."*

In the border states of Virginia, Arkansas, Tennessee, and North Carolina, though, the North's response to Fort Sumter convinced the previously uncommitted border states of Virginia, Arkansas, North Carolina, and Tennessee that their future lay with their fellow slave states in the Deep South. They all seceded by early June, and the city of Richmond, Virginia—located only 100 miles from the federal capital of Washington, D.C.—was established as the new capital of the Confederacy.

Lincoln and the North moved swiftly to keep the remaining four slave states—Delaware, Maryland, Kentucky, and Missouri—out of the clutches of the Confederacy. Lincoln was not worried about Delaware, which remained staunchly pro-Union despite its slavery practices. The other three states, though, contained many people who were openly enthusiastic about secession and hostile to Lincoln (in the 1860 election for example, Lincoln received less than 3 percent of the vote in Maryland). Lincoln used a blend of political pressure, arrests of pro-secession lawmakers, and martial law to keep Maryland, Missouri, and Kentucky in Union hands. However, large numbers of men from all three states traveled southward with horse and rifle to join the Confederate Army.

An engraving showing the bombardment of Fort Sumter by Confederate batteries.

Finally, Lincoln and Congress moved to carve a new pro-Union state out of the mountains of western Virginia, where struggling white farmers had little use for the wealthy and politically powerful slave owners in the state's eastern reaches. West Virginia was a slave state upon its admission in June 1863, but as a condition of statehood it agreed to several provisions that would gradually abolish all slavery within its borders.

## Building Armies

When the first shots of the Civil War were fired at Fort Sumter in April 1861, the United States' existing army amounted to only about 16,000 men, most of whom were stationed in remote Western territories to protect settlers from Indians. The federal navy had been neglected for years as well, with fewer than 50 ships and 9,000 sailors at its immediate disposal in early 1861. But although these military resources were small and weak, Lincoln and Congress knew that they could be bolstered quickly. After all, the North bristled with big

A Union army recruiting tent at a park in New York City.

factories and shipyards, an extensive rail and water transportation network, and millions of able-bodied young men.

In the spring of 1861 the Union launched major campaigns to ready its armed forces for war. The navy bought merchant and passenger ships by the dozen and carried out an ambitious warship construction program. By the end of the war in 1865, the Union Navy had more than 670 ships and 24,000 officers and enlisted men under its command. The Union Army underwent similar expansion as the War Department collaborated with state officials to absorb new soldiers and outfit them with the rifles, ammunition, food, blankets, canteens, cannons, horses, and other materials they needed. By early 1862, more than 700,000 men had joined the Union army, most of them for two- or three-year terms. These soldiers were assigned to several different federal fighting forces, the largest of which became the Army of the Potomac. As it turned out, it proved much easier for the Union to increase the size of its army than to organize an effective supply system for its troops. As Lincoln acknowledged in his July 4, 1861, message to Congress, "one of the greatest perplexities of the government is to avoid receiving troops faster than it can provide for them."

The Confederacy, meanwhile, authorized a call for 400,000 additional volunteers for one- to three-year terms in mid-1861. It had fewer white men available to answer this call, however, and arming slaves for the war was out of the question. By mid-1862 the Confederate Army had managed to grow to only 200,000-250,000 soldiers. It added another 200,000 or so before the year was out, but the Union kept at least a two-to-one advantage in troop strength for the remainder of the war. Since the South had few factories, shipyards, and railroads, it also struggled to build an effective navy and procure rifles, tents, uniforms, bandages, and other materials in the necessary quantities. The main silver lining for the Confederacy in its military preparations was its great success in attracting talented officers from the ranks of the federal army and the nation's leading military schools.

## The Union Makes the First Move

As the Union and Confederate armies organized themselves in the spring of 1861, Lincoln approved a naval blockade of all Southern ports to prevent the rebels from getting military supplies from Europe or black market dealers in the North. This strategy had been advanced by General-in-Chief Winfield Scott, who claimed that starving the South of supplies would work better than a full-scale invasion, especially since the federal army that was being created was so untested in battle. Scott's proposed blockade came to be known as the Anaconda Plan, after the snake known for crushing its prey in its coils.

This strategy was not aggressive enough for most Northerners, though. Their roaring calls for a full invasion echoed through the White House, Congress, and the War Department, and in July the Lincoln administration gave in. On July 16, 35,000 troops marching under the banner of the Union's Army of Northeastern Virginia moved down into Virginia under the command of General Irvin McDowell and united with a 15,000-strong force led by General Robert Patterson. Their target was a Confederate force that had been stationed to defend Manassas Junction, home of a railroad junction that connected the farmlands of Virginia's Shenandoah Valley to the cities of the Deep South. This 20,000-troop rebel force was commanded by General P. G. T. Beauregard, who had overseen the capture of Fort Sumter a few months earlier.

On July 21 these armies clashed in the first major battle of the Civil War. This battle, known as the First Battle of Bull Run in the North and the First Battle of Manassas in the South, was marked by confusion and chaos. "It was the first taste

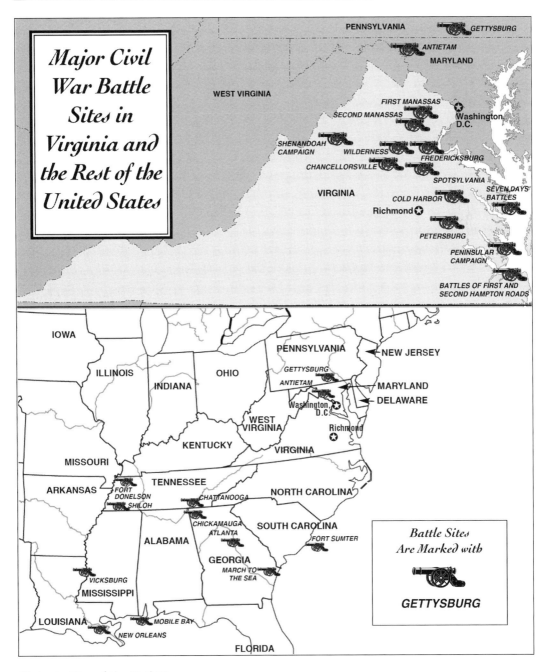

*Major Civil War Battle Sites in Virginia and the Rest of the United States*

PENNSYLVANIA — GETTYSBURG
ANTIETAM
MARYLAND
WEST VIRGINIA
FIRST MANASSAS
SECOND MANASSAS
Washington, D.C.
SHENANDOAH CAMPAIGN
WILDERNESS
CHANCELLORSVILLE
FREDERICKSBURG
SPOTSYLVANIA
VIRGINIA
COLD HARBOR
SEVEN DAYS' BATTLES
Richmond
PETERSBURG
PENINSULAR CAMPAIGN
BATTLES OF FIRST AND SECOND HAMPTON ROADS

IOWA
PENNSYLVANIA
NEW JERSEY
ILLINOIS
OHIO
INDIANA
GETTYSBURG
ANTIETAM
MARYLAND
DELAWARE
Washington, D.C.
WEST VIRGINIA
Richmond
KENTUCKY
VIRGINIA
MISSOURI
ARKANSAS
TENNESSEE
FORT DONELSON
SHILOH
CHATTANOOGA
NORTH CAROLINA
CHICKAMAUGA
ATLANTA
SOUTH CAROLINA
ALABAMA
FORT SUMTER
GEORGIA
MARCH TO THE SEA
VICKSBURG
MISSISSIPPI
LOUISIANA
MOBILE BAY
NEW ORLEANS
FLORIDA

*Battle Sites Are Marked with*

**GETTYSBURG**

Major battles of the Civil War.

31

of combat for almost everyone—and it showed," said Civil War historian James M. McPherson. "Men attacked in groups rather than in lines. Some men accidentally shot their comrades. Others became so excited during the battle that they forgot to fire their rifles; they just kept reloading."[1] The confusion was further worsened by the fact that each side wore outfits of different colors, making it hard to identify who was an ally and who was an enemy. This problem became apparent in subsequent battles as well, and it eventually convinced the Union to pick blue as its standard uniform color and the Confederacy to outfit its troops in gray.

The First Battle of Bull Run ended in a resounding defeat for the Union after 10,000 Confederate troops commanded by General Joseph E. Johnston provided reinforcements to Beauregard. The loss was all the more humiliating because Union soldiers were joined in their retreat by panicked civilians from the capital who had gathered nearby to watch what they thought would be a great victory for the North.

The First Battle of Bull Run gave the South a big boost in confidence. It also shook the North's expectations that the war would be quickly and easily won. In response, Lincoln signed a bill to organize 500,000 volunteers to serve three-year military terms. The president and military officials also added several other armies to the Army of Northeastern Virginia and named the reconstituted force the Army of the Potomac. Command of the massive army—the largest in the entire Union arsenal—was given to General George B. McClellan. On November 1, 1861, McClellan also replaced the retiring Scott as commander of the entire Union Army.

The rest of 1861 passed quietly, but both sides knew that 1862 would bring a new round of clashes. As winter set in both armies worked hard to get themselves ready. They prepared defenses, finalized their command structures, drilled their young troops in various aspects of battle, and stockpiled supplies for the coming storm. Down in Richmond, though, these preparations were overshadowed by a tense debate over whether the Confederacy should institute a military draft to fill the ranks of its army. President Davis and some members of the Confederate Congress supported a bill that would make it mandatory for Southern white males between the ages of eighteen and thirty-five to serve a three-year enlistment as a Confederate soldier. The proposal was strongly opposed, though, by many Southerners. Some objected to the bill because of a provision that allowed wealthy whites to hire replacements to serve in their place. Others complained that the Conscription Act, as it was called, trampled on individual freedoms.

The first major land battle of the war, known as the First Battle of Bull Run or First Manassas, ended in a decisive victory for the Confederates.

## The War Resumes

A mere five weeks after the New Year, the sounds of rifle fire and cannon blasts once again blared across the continent. The action first erupted in western Tennessee, where federal troops under the command of General Ulysses S. Grant captured two strategically important rebel forts located on the Cumberland and Tennessee Rivers. His victories at Fort Henry on February 6 and Fort Donelson on February 16 gave the North a clear pathway into the heart of Dixie, as the South was sometimes called. By the end of the month Union forces under the command of General Henry W. Halleck had made their way down the Cumberland and captured Nashville, Tennessee's largest city.

News of these events struck fear in the hearts of people across the Confederacy. It also broke down resistance to the military draft that was being pushed by Davis and his allies. "The enemy are in some portions of almost every state in the Confederacy," declared Texas senator Louis Wigfall. "We need a large

Ulysses S. Grant's successes in western Tennessee heartened disillusioned Northerners.

army. How are you going to get it [other than through a draft]?"[2] This argument eventually carried the day, and the Conscription Act became law on April 16, 1862. By the end of 1862 the Conscription Act had increased the total size of the Confederate Army to about 450,000 troops. Few of these soldiers were wealthy slave owners, though; in October 1862 the Confederate government added an amendment that exempted all white men who owned twenty or more slaves from the draft.

Grant's victories at Fort Henry and Fort Donelson, meanwhile, made him the Union's first major war hero. The capture of the two forts also convinced the War Department to promote him to the rank of major general. After receiving command of a 48,000-troop force that came to be known as the Army of the Tennessee, Grant was ordered by Halleck to advance deeper into Tennessee. He moved his army steadily forward, and by early April Grant was perched near the northern border of Mississippi. Waiting for reinforcements from Nashville before advancing into Mississippi, Grant set up an encampment on the west bank of the Tennessee River near a country church known as Shiloh to local residents.

Grant assumed that his army was in no danger, but on the morning of April 6, 40,000 rebel troops led by General Albert Sidney Johnston burst out of the surrounding woods. Grant and his men were driven from their camp, but they made a desperate stand at a stretch of rural road that came to be known as the Hornet's Nest. As the bloody battle continued, Johnston was killed and P. G. T. Beauregard assumed command of the Confederate force. The day's battle ended with neither side gaining a decisive edge, but on the night of April 6 Grant's reinforcements arrived. Armed with these fresh new troops, Grant orchestrated a brutal counterattack the following day that forced Beauregard to call a retreat. Grant declined to take pursuit, though, for the two-day battle had taken a fearsome toll on his army. He later commented that by the time the battlefield fell silent, it contained so many corpses that "it would have been possible to walk across the clearing in any direction stepping on dead bodies without a foot touching the ground."[3] Grant was not exaggerating, for the Battle of Shiloh was the deadliest battle in American history to that point. About 13,000 Union troops and 10,000 Confederate soldiers were killed or wounded in the clash.

## The Battle of New Orleans

Eleven days after the Battle of Shiloh concluded, another major showdown erupted between federal and rebel forces. This clash was for control of New Orleans, Louisiana, a large and strategically vital port city located on the Gulf of Mexico near the mouth of the Mississippi River.

On April 18 a Union Navy fleet under the command of Admiral David G. Farragut cruised up the entrance of the river to within range of two forts that defended the city's southern approach. Farragut spent the next several days raining artillery shells on the forts, but neither outpost fell. Instead, the cannons of both forts kept vigil over the river, ready to lay waste to any vessels that tried to pass.

Farragut thus forged a new scheme to break the stalemate. Early on the morning of April 24, Farragut's fleet of seventeen warships quietly began moving upriver under cover of darkness. When Confederate lookouts belatedly discovered the movement, the forts sent down a furious hail of cannon fire. They were aided by rebel tugboats anchored further upstream. The tugboats released flaming rafts into the current in hopes that they would float down and collide with the oncoming federal ships. Farragut's fleet evaded most of the rafts, however, and the nighttime made it very hard for the forts to find targets for their cannons. After Farragut pushed through the one-mile gauntlet (losing four of his seventeen warships in the process) he had clear sailing to New Orleans. He arrived there the next day and quickly took command of the city.

## The Peninsular Campaign

Although the first months of 1862 were not kind to the Confederate military in the war's "Western Theater"—the country west of the Appalachians—the rebels had better luck in the East. As the main Union force in the Eastern Theatre, McClellan's Army of the Potomac had the capacity to make a run at Richmond. If McClellan could capture the rebel capital, it would be a shattering blow to the Confederacy. Yet McClellan kept training and drilling his troops long after Lincoln had wanted him to leave Washington. The president

The Union navy's April 1862 victory at New Orleans pried the lower reaches of the Mississippi River out of the grip of the Confederacy.

became so disgusted that he remarked that "if General McClellan does not want to use the army, I would like to borrow it for a time."[4]

McClellan did not order his army forward until March 14, a few days after Lincoln stripped him of his duties as general-in-chief of the Union Army (the position was left vacant until July, when Halleck was appointed to fill the spot). McClellan left 40,000 men behind to defend Washington from Confederate forces in the region. He was particularly concerned by Thomas "Stonewall" Jackson, who spent the spring of 1862 running circles around Union forces in Virginia's Shenandoah Valley. McClellan assured the remaining 110,000 soldiers who would accompany McClellan on his campaign against Richmond that he loved them "from the depths of his heart," and that he would watch over them "as a parent over his children."[5]

McClellan transported his army by boat down Chesapeake Bay to the eastern tip of a Virginia peninsula between the York and James Rivers. The troops disembarked and began their advance toward Richmond, but McClellan's offensive—which came to be known as the Peninsular Campaign—then slowed to a crawl. The cautious McClellan halted his advance when a small Confederate force further up the peninsula convinced him that it was actually an army equal to his own. This trick was engineered by Confederate major general John Bankhead Magruder, who "kept up a sporadic, widely scattered artillery barrage, ordered his bandsmen to play loudly after dark, and paraded one battalion in and out of a clearing in an endless circle until it seemed to Union observers a mighty host."[6]

McClellan sent a telegram back to Washington explaining his decision to halt the advance until he could gather further reinforcements, but Lincoln responded to the general's caution with exasperation. "By delay the enemy will relatively gain upon you—that is, he will gain faster, by *fortifications* and *reinforcements*, than you can by re-inforcements alone," Lincoln wrote back. "It is indispensable to you that you strike a blow.... *You must act.*"[7] As Lincoln feared, the general's slow progress gave Confederate forces under General Joseph E. Johnston weeks of additional time to shore up Richmond's defenses.

McClellan finally approached the far outskirts of Richmond at the end of May. It was here, at a village called Fair Oaks, that the Army of the Potomac finally engaged in its first serious clashes with Johnston's Army of Northern Virginia. When Johnston was wounded during the battle, he was replaced by General Robert E. Lee, whose cunning leadership over the war's next few years would make him a famous figure in American history (see Lee biography, p. 138).

The earliest foundations of the Lee legend were laid a month after he took command of the Army of Northern Virginia. McClellan's fears of defeat kept

Major General George B. McClellan commanded the Army of the Potomac during its 1862 Peninsular Campaign.

General Robert E. Lee's maneuvers during the Seven Days' Battles forced McClellan to retreat out of Virginia.

the Army of the Potomac idle through the first weeks of June, even though it was camped only about twenty miles from Richmond. Lee used this time to orchestrate a battle plan to chase McClellan and his troops back to Washington. On June 25 Lee set his strategy in motion, sending his 90,000 rebel troops against the Army of the Potomac. For the next week the battle raged, with the North continually giving ground. On July 1 the so-called Seven Days' Battles finally came to an end when McClellan ordered a complete withdrawal. The news that the hated Yankees no longer menaced Richmond sparked joy and celebration across the Confederacy. "[Lee] has established his reputation forever," declared one Richmond newspaper, "and has entitled himself to the lasting gratitude of his country."[8]

## Lee Presses His Advantage

The Seven Days' Battles convinced Lincoln and his war advisors to make major changes. They gave Halleck overall command of the Union Army and arranged for General John Pope to head a new army—the Army of Virginia—cobbled together out of several smaller forces. Halleck devised a plan to combine the resources of Pope and McClellan into a single army to penetrate deep into the Confederacy and overwhelm Lee.

Before this plan could be executed, though, Lee decided to take the fight to the North. First, he sent a contingent of his Army of Northern Virginia to confront Pope in Virginia. Part of this force, under the command of General Thomas J. "Stonewall" Jackson, got in a fierce battle with Pope's army on August 9 at Cedar Mountain, Virginia. Jackson's 25,000-man army then seized a Union supply depot at Manassas Junction, where the First Battle of Bull Run had been fought a year earlier. Stunned and embarrassed, Pope turned his army to Manassas, and on August 29 he launched a major attack on the rebel position. Jackson's troops were well dug in, however, and they resisted the onslaught until reinforcements sent by Lee arrived. This infusion of Confederate troops, commanded by General James Longstreet, went unnoticed by Pope and his officers.

When Pope awoke on the morning of August 30 he was convinced that he was on the verge of a great victory. He accurately sensed that Jackson's soldiers could not hold out much longer against his much larger Union force. Pope thus ordered another full-scale assault—only to have Longstreet's undetected troops rake its left flank with deadly barrages of artillery and rifle fire. Pope was forced to withdraw his badly wounded army, which suffered an estimated 16,000 casualties in the clash. Lee's army, by contrast, had only a little more

General Thomas "Stonewall" Jackson emerged as one of Lee's most trusted generals during the summer and fall of 1862.

than half that number of killed or wounded in what came to be known as the Second Battle of Bull Run or Second Battle of Manassas.

Pope's terrible defeat at Manassas—and his abrasive personality, which had made him unpopular among his own men—convinced Lincoln and the War Department to relieve him of command. Pope was sent out west to fight Indians and command of his army was transferred to McClellan. This solution did not make the Lincoln White House particularly happy, but the president consoled himself that McClellan's well-known concern for his soldiers' safety might improve the army's sagging morale.

## The Battle of Antietam

Fresh off his victory at Manassas, Lee marched his Army of Northern Virginia across the Potomac River and into Maryland. His plan was to cut a wide swath through the North, feeding and supplying his army from the fields, pasturelands, and armories of the Yankees. He thought such a campaign might convince Great Britain and France to recognize Confederate nationhood—and that it could demoralize the North to the point that it would give up its attempts to force the South back into the United States.

When word of Lee's advance reached Washington, McClellan and his Army of the Potomac were sent west to head him off. On September 13 a Union soldier stumbled upon a copy of Lee's plan to attack a Union railroad depot at Harrisburg in southern Pennsylvania. The papers, which were stuffed in an envelope and wrapped around three cigars, must have been lost by a Confederate officer. The paper, which historians came to call "Lost Order 191," also included other valuable information, such as the travel routes of various wings of Lee's command. It noted, for example, that half of Lee's army was with Stonewall Jackson, who had been ordered to carry out a raid against a federal armory at Harper's Ferry, Virginia, just across the Potomac River.

This secret information gave McClellan a tremendous opportunity to swoop in and wipe out the undermanned Lee. The Union commander recognized his good fortune. "Here is a paper with which, if I cannot whip Bobbie Lee, I will be willing to go home!"[9] he proclaimed. Once again, however, McClellan's fear of losing his own soldiers kept him from taking advantage of the opportunity to strike a harsh blow against the enemy. McClellan had 75,000 troops with him even after sending 20,000 soldiers to Harper's Ferry (they failed to arrive in time to stop Jackson's successful raid). Meanwhile, Lee had fewer than 20,000 troops. But conflicting reports from scouts convinced McClellan that the Confederate force was even greater than his own. The risk-averse general thus wasted hours coming up with a needlessly complicated plan of attack. Eighteen hours passed between the time that McClellan read the contents of Lost Order 191 and the time that he ordered the Army of the Potomac forward.

By September 16 McClellan and his entire Army of the Potomac had reached the vicinity of Antietam Creek outside of Sharpsburg, Maryland. This was the site of Lee's encampment, and the rebels watched the gathering enemy with mounting dismay. "The number increased, and larger and larger grew the field of blue until it seemed to stretch as far as the eye could see,"[10] said Longstreet. But McClellan decided to wait until the following morning—the 17th—to attack. This delay saved Lee's army, for it was not until the night of the 16th that Stonewall Jackson and his 20,000 men completed their return trip from Harper's Ferry. When Jackson rejoined Lee he instantly doubled the size of the general's army—though the Confederates were still outnumbered by almost two to one.

Fallen Confederate soldiers after the titanic Battle of Antietam.

McClellan finally gave the order to attack on the morning of September 17. All day the two armies fought, soaking the battleground with their blood as they waged desperate combat over every woodland, hill, and ridge around Antietam Creek. By the time the rifles and artillery fell silent that night, more than 23,000 Union and Confederate soldiers had been killed or wounded. The Battle of Antietam thus became the single bloodiest day in the history of the war. The next day passed quietly, with both sides glaring at each other from their fortifications as they tended their thousands of wounded. That night—September 18—Lee quietly withdrew his battered Army of Northern Virginia from the battlefield and began the journey back to Virginia.

## Lincoln Issues the Emancipation Proclamation

The Battle of Antietam was a lost opportunity for the Union. Nonetheless, it was a victory of sorts. McClellan had halted the Southern offensive into the North and badly damaged Lee's army. Lincoln capitalized on this moment to make a proclamation that dramatically changed the complexion of the entire war.

Back in June Congress had passed a law forbidding slavery anywhere in the western territories, thus settling an issue that had tied the United States in knots for half a century. On September 22 Lincoln built on this law by issuing the Emancipation Proclamation, which declared that unless the seceded Confederate states came back to the Union by January 1, 1863, all of their slaves would be free. The proclamation also called for blacks to be admitted into the federal military, albeit in segregated units.

The people of the Confederacy ridiculed the declaration, pointing out that the federal government had no way to enforce it in the South. But their dismissal missed the point. By explicitly framing the war not only as a crusade to preserve the Union, but also as an effort to extend American principles of freedom and liberty to blacks, Lincoln made it impossible for Great Britain or France to extend recognition to the Confederacy. In fact, the Emancipation Proclamation increased European sympathy for the Union cause. "The triumph of the Confederacy would be a victory of the powers of evil," wrote the influential English philosopher John Stuart Mill in response to the proclamation. "[It] would give courage to the enemies of progress and damp the spirits of friends all over the civilized world."[11]

The Emancipation Proclamation was not applauded by everyone in the North. Lincoln's Democratic opponents charged that it would further lengthen the war, which had already gone on far longer than most Northerners had anticipated. Some abolitionists also criticized the president for failing to include slaves living in Union slave states. But the famous black abolitionist Frederick Douglass spoke of "shout[ing] for joy that we live to record this righteous decree," and the move shored up sagging Northern enthusiasm for the war. Both civilians and soldiers seemed to respond to Lincoln's claim that the North was now carrying the torch for humankind's highest ideals of justice and liberty.

Finally, the Emancipation Proclamation convinced tens of thousands of blacks to take up arms for the Union. As word of the proclamation trickled down into the Deep South, many male slaves fled the cotton fields for the North. Historians estimate that as many as 200,000 former slaves eventually fought in the Civil War under the American flag.

## The Battle of Fredericksburg

The Emancipation Proclamation, though, could not mask the federal armed forces' continued struggles on the battlefield. Over in the West, where the Union had gained a lot of territory earlier in the year, federal troops steadi-

Rebel soldiers fire from behind stone walls at the Battle of Fredericksburg, which ended in another decisive victory for Lee.

ly lost ground. Quick-striking Confederate cavalry units constantly tormented Union supply lines and arms depots, and in the fall Confederate general Braxton Bragg and his Army of Mississippi managed to capture Kentucky's capital of Lexington from a Yankee garrison and install a secessionist governor. Bragg's triumph was brief; within a matter of weeks he had retreated back into Tennessee. Nonetheless, Northern dissatisfaction with the war's progress badly hurt Lincoln's Republicans in the November 1862 elections. The Democratic Party, which relentlessly attacked the president as an incompetent commander in chief, kept their majorities in both the U.S. Senate and House of Representatives and won the governorships of several states.

Once the elections were over, Lincoln once again removed McClellan from command of the Army of the Potomac. McClellan's dismissal came after he failed to obey Lincoln's instructions to carry out another offensive into Virginia after Antietam. McClellan's replacement was General Ambrose E. Burnside, who quickly made plans for another march on Richmond.

Burnside and more than 130,000 soldiers in the Army of the Potomac made their way through Virginia to a spot on the Rappahannock River directly opposite the town of Fredericksburg. Burnside's plans called for the War Department to send pontoon bridges to Fredericksburg so that his huge army could cross the river there and continue southward to Richmond. But delivery of the bridges was delayed by two weeks, enabling various detachments of Lee's Army of Northern Virginia to catch up to Burnside. By the time the bridges arrived, Lee and 75,000 battle-hardened rebel troops had dug themselves into strong defensive positions on the Fredericksburg side of the river.

On December 13 Burnside attacked. All day long, he sent wave after wave of Union troops against the rebels. Lee's forces, though, occupied extremely advantageous positions. Their cannons looked out from hilltops over fields that provided no cover for Yankee soldiers, and their rifles bristled from behind long stone walls. The Confederates thus were able to smash each wave before it could breach their defenses. Burnside did not abandon his stubborn plan of frontal attack until nightfall. The following day he retreated from Fredericksburg and headed back to Washington in humiliation. His foolish battle strategy had resulted in 12,600 Union casualties. The Army of Northern Virginia, by contrast, lost 5,300 men to death or wounding.

When the American Civil War started, soldiers and civilians of the North had been confident of a swift and decisive victory. By the time of Burnside's defeat at Fredericksburg, many of them just wanted to put the year behind them. "As I look back on 1862 I am bewildered when I think of the hundreds of miles I have tramped, the thousands of dead and wounded that I have seen," wrote Union officer Elisha Hunt Rhodes in a New Year's Eve 1862 diary entry. "The year has not amounted to much as far as the War is concerned, but we hope for the best and feel sure that in the end the Union will be restored. Goodbye, 1862."[12]

## Notes

[1] McPherson, James M. *Fields of Fury: The American Civil War.* New York: Atheneum, 2002, p. 18.

[2] Quoted in McPherson, James M. *Battle Cry of Freedom: The Civil War Era.* New York: Oxford University Press, 1988, p. 430.

[3] Grant, Ulysses S. *Personal Memoirs of Ulysses S. Grant.* 1885-1886. Reprint. New York: Cosimo, 2007, p. 138.

[4] McPherson, James M. *Tried by War: Abraham Lincoln as Commander in Chief.* New York: Penguin Press, 2008, p. 66.

[5] Quoted in "Important from Washington: Stirring Address from Gen. McClellan to his Army." *New York Times,* March 16, 1862. Retrieved from http://www.nytimes.com/1862/03/16/news/important-washington-stirring-address-gen-mcclellan-his-army-time-for-inaction.html?pagewanted=all.

remove his army all the way to southern Tennessee. This withdrawal gave Union or Federal forces control over much of the state's middle section.

Meanwhile, President Abraham Lincoln and his War Department were determined to conquer the Confederate-controlled cities of Port Hudson, Louisiana, and Vicksburg, Mississippi, both of which sat on the banks of the Mississippi River. They directed Grant to take the heavily fortified towns, which were the only remaining obstacles to complete Union control of the entire length of the waterway. Once these towns fell, Yankee forces would be able to freely transport troops and supplies up and down the river. Victories over Vicksburg and Port Hudson would also enable the North to isolate Confederate states west of the river from those in the East. "Vicksburg is the key!" declared Lincoln. "The war can never be brought to a close until that key is in our pocket."[3]

As Grant mobilized his army to head south, General Henry W. Halleck, who at that time was overall commander of all the Union armies, wrote him a note of encouragement. "The eyes and hopes of the whole country are directed at your army," stated Halleck. "In my opinion, the opening of the Mississippi River will be to us of more advantage than the capture of forty Richmonds."[4]

> *"Here we see the horrors of dreadful war! War knows no Sabbath. I thought of the quiet Sabbaths at home and contrasted them with the noise and din of war that was now raging all around us. I thought, will I ever see those peaceful days again?"*
> *– A Southern chaplain during the Siege of Vicksburg*

## Marching on Vicksburg

The main prize sought by Grant was Vicksburg, which was defended by nearly 20,000 Confederate troops under the command of Lieutenant General John C. Pemberton. The city was situated atop high bluffs that looked over the river, and Pemberton's troops manned a fearsome line of defenses that included forts, trenches, gunpits, redoubts and other stone, brick, and earthwork constructions. Grant knew that prying the Rebels out of these positions was going to be a miserable and bloody undertaking, even though he had a much larger army at his disposal.

Grant and his army of 40,000 troops set out for Vicksburg in late March. After a month of hard marching down the western side of the Mississippi, Grant reached Bruinsburg, which lay about 30 miles south of Vicksburg. Here he rendezvoused with a Union fleet under the command of Admiral David D. Porter.

## Military Organization of
## Union and Confederate Armies in the Civil War

During the Civil War, the militaries of both the North and South were composed of small units that, when joined together in various and ever-larger configurations, formed armies. Both the Federal and Confederate armies featured six basic units of organization:

*Company* — up to 100 men, commanded by a captain.

*Regiment* — a grouping of ten companies, commanded by a colonel. Regiments could technically include as many as 1,000 troops, but due to battlefield losses and sickness, some Civil War regiments only had 500-800 men. Smaller versions of regiments composed of four to eight companies were sometimes called battalions. Cavalries on both sides were generally organized into regiments of ten to twelve companies.

*Brigade* — a unit of four to six regiments, commanded by a brigadier general.

*Division* — a unit of three to four regiments (though Confederate divisions sometimes had five or even more), commanded by a brigadier general or major general; a full division could contain as many as 12,000 troops.

*Corps* — a group of three or more divisions, often supplemented with units such as artillery batteries, commanded by a major general.

*Army* — a grouping of from one to as many as eight corps, commanded by a major general or lieutenant general. Whereas Union armies were frequently named after rivers and waterways (i.e., Army of the Potomac, Army of the Mississippi), Confederate armies received their names from their state or geographic area of origin (i.e., Army of Northern Virginia, Army of Tennessee).

The Union ships transported Grant's Army of the Tennessee over to the eastern side of the river. After disembarking, Grant carved a course inland, moving steadily to the northeast.

This route had several strategic advantages. The presence of the Big Black River on Grant's left flank lessened his vulnerability to attack. The Union army's path also enabled it to capture and raze the town of Jackson and sever railroad lines that connected Vicksburg with supply centers further east. Grant's presence also kept Confederate reinforcements commanded by General Joseph E. Johnston from linking up with Pemberton's troops in Vicksburg. Finally, Grant knew that if he could attack Vicksburg from the high terrain east of the city rather than the lower approaches from the west or south, he would be able to neutralize the Confederate army's "high ground" military advantage.

In mid-May Grant pivoted back toward Vicksburg. Marching on the town from the east, his superior forces overwhelmed Confederate troops in several minor battles. By May 18 he had arranged his troops in a semi-circle around the city's northern, eastern, and southern flanks. These maneuvers kept Pemberton's isolated troops pinned against the Mississippi, which was under Union control both upstream and downstream of Vicksburg. On May 19 and again on May 22 Grant ordered full-scale assaults against the Vicksburg fortifications. Neither attack was able to fully breach Pemberton's defenses, though. Grant's Army of the Tennessee had to retreat each time, and it lost 4,000 men to death or injury in the two offensives.

## The Siege of Vicksburg

At this point, Grant changed tactics. Rather than order yet another costly assault on Vicksburg—an assault that would surely claim the lives of many of his troops and possibly be just as unsuccessful as the first two offensives—the Union general decided to lay siege to the city. The siege formally began on May 26. Over the next six weeks his army kept all food, ammunition, medical aid, and other supplies from the outside world from reaching the city.

This slow strangulation had its desired effect. "Throughout June," noted one account of the blockade, "the gallant, but weary, defenders of Vicksburg suffered from reduced rations, exposure to the elements, and constant bombardment of enemy guns. Reduced in number by sickness and battle casualties, the garrison of Vicksburg was spread dangerously thin. Soldiers and citizens alike began to despair that help would ever come."[5] In the meantime, Grant steadily added to his army with reinforcements, bolstering the size of the force under his command to more than 70,000 troops. He also laid siege to nearby Port Hudson, which by late May was surrounded by troops under the command of Union major general Nathaniel P. Banks.

Vicksburg's main hope for rescue was Johnston and his army of 24,000 men, who remained in western Mississippi. Johnston wanted further rein-

Grant's Siege of Vicksburg was a devastating blow to Confederate operations in the West.

forcements before he engaged Grant. By late June, however, civilians and soldiers trapped in Vicksburg were eating family pets to survive, and the medical situation had become ghastly. "On passing through the hospital what a heart-rending spectacle greets the eyes!" wrote one Confederate army chaplain. "Here we see the horrors of dreadful war! ... Why should I proceed any further? Every part of the body is pierced. All conceivable wounds are inflicted.... There is no Sabbath quiet here. War knows no Sabbath. I thought of the quiet Sabbaths at home and contrasted them with the noise and din of war that was now raging all around us. I thought, will I ever see those peaceful days again?"[6]

On June 28 Pemberton received a letter from a group of anonymous Confederate soldiers that urged him to accept defeat. "If you can't feed us, you had better surrender, horrible as the idea is, than suffer this noble army to disgrace themselves by desertion,"[7] stated the note. Pemberton recoiled at the idea of surrendering, but he also recognized that he had no other option. On July 4 he formally surrendered the city to Grant and his army. As Union forces moved into the conquered city, they distributed desperately needed food and medical supplies to the populace. When the Confederate garrison at Port Hudson learned of Vicksburg's fall, it too surrendered, on July 9. The entire length and breadth of the mighty Mississippi was now in Union hands.

Grant's Army of the Tennessee took possession of all the enemy guns, ammunition, and artillery in Vicksburg, but the victorious Grant also offered general "parole" to the 29,000 soldiers he had captured in the city. Under this system, which was widely practiced by both sides during the war's first two years, Confederate soldiers were allowed to leave Vicksburg and avoid becoming prisoners of war. In return, they promised not to take up arms against the U.S. government until they were officially exchanged for an enemy captive of equal rank. This offer has sometimes been described as a generous gesture by Grant, but other historians point out that transporting, feeding, and guarding so many enemy prisoners at once would have been a nightmare for his Army of the Tennessee.

## The Battle of Chancellorsville

Grant's triumph at Vicksburg added to his growing reputation as the North's most valuable and talented general. Back east, however, the Union's efforts to outwit and outfight the *South's* most valuable and talented general—Robert E. Lee—produced only embarrassment and sorrow for the North during the early months of 1863.

In January 1863 General Ambrose Burnside mobilized his Army of the Potomac in an offensive against Lee and his Army of Northern Virginia. Lee and his Confederate troops remained in the vicinity of Fredericksburg, Virginia, where they had delivered a sound thrashing to the Army of the Potomac only a month previous. Burnside badly wanted to repair his damaged reputation and seize some momentum for the North, but the weather refused to cooperate with his scheme. Heavy rainstorms turned roadways into sodden quagmires. Scores of supply and artillery wagons became stranded in the mud, which also made it virtually impossible for Burnside's infantry to advance. By January 23 Burnside reluctantly conceded that his campaign had deteriorated into a grim "mud march." He ordered the Army of the Potomac to reverse course and head back to their winter quarters. This sequence of events was so humiliating to the Lincoln administration and the U.S. Army as a whole that Burnside was sacked on January 25. His place at the helm of the Army of the Potomac was taken by Major General Joseph Hooker.

Union general Joseph Hooker vowed to use the Army of the Potomac to smash Lee once and for all.

Hooker's administrative abilities and cocky nature gave a much-needed boost to the army's morale and fighting capacity. By April, when Hooker launched a new military campaign against Lee, the troops under his command were eager to redeem themselves on the field of battle. They cheered when word filtered through the ranks that Hooker had told his senior officers that "my plans are perfect, and when I start to carry them out, may God have mercy on General Lee, for I will have none."[8]

As the Army of the Potomac advanced on Fredericksburg, where Lee's army remained, Hooker sent a huge detachment of cavalry into the countryside between Fredericksburg and Richmond, thus cutting Lee off from communication with the Confederate capital. Hooker then divided his remaining force of 130,000 federal troops into two armies of roughly equal size. Hooker placed one of his armies around Fredericksburg to occupy Lee's attention. He then sent the other one around Lee's left flank to the west. The Union general's plan was to crush the Confederate foe in a pincer movement— a pinching or squeezing maneuver in which both flanks of an enemy are attacked simultaneously. At the very least, Hooker intended to make sure that Lee's army would no longer threaten the North with invasion. If the campaign went as Hooker hoped and he was able to engage the Army of Northern Virginia, he might even be able to cripple the South's largest army permanently.

Lee and his chief officers knew that their Army of Northern Virginia, which was outnumbered by more than two to one, was in grave peril if it stayed in the region. But if Lee obeyed conventional military wisdom and withdrew to the south, the Confederacy's morale, momentum, and territorial advantage would all be diminished. With those considerations in mind, Lee devised a daring plan. He left 10,000 troops in Fredericksburg, then raced to meet Hooker's column to the west with his remaining 50,000 men. Meanwhile, an advance guard of Rebel cavalry under the command of Thomas "Stonewall" Jackson harassed Hooker's western column to the point that the Union general called a halt to his advance. Fooled by Jackson's aggressive stance, Hooker adopted a defensive

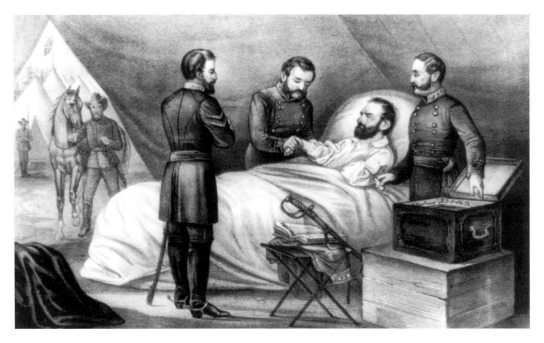

This Currier & Ives print depicts the final hours of Thomas "Stonewall" Jackson.

position around Chancellorsville, a remote hamlet that featured a mansion-like brick tavern and little else.

Hooker's decision to halt the advance and dig in at Chancellorsville was greeted with disbelief by Union field commanders. They believed that Hooker's caution was costing the army a golden opportunity to strike the enemy at a time and place of its own choosing. "To hear from his own lip that the advantages gained by the successful marches of his lieutenants were to culminate in fighting a defensive battle in that nest of thickets was too much, and I retired from his presence with the belief that my commanding general was a whipped man,"[9] wrote Major General Darius N. Crouch.

Hooker's halt gave Lee the time he needed to reach Chancellorsville and implement his own attack strategy. Armed with intelligence from Confederate cavalry that the Army of the Potomac's right flank was only lightly fortified, Lee and Jackson stayed up until the early hours of May 2 examining various military options. Lee eventually decided on an audacious plan that pivoted on his conviction that Hooker had lost his nerve and would not go on the attack. Lee kept about 14,000 troops with him at Chancellorsville, but he directed Jackson to take virtually all the rest of his army, sneak over to the Union's right side undetected, then launch a mighty blow aimed at caving in the right flank of Hooker's force.

If Hooker had taken the initiative over the next 24 hours and launched an offensive against Lee's small and thinly spread force, the Army of the Potomac could have easily taken Chancellorsville—and destroyed Lee's column in the process. Hooker stayed put, though. Jackson, on the other hand, reached his desired position on the afternoon of May 2 after a twelve-mile march through the wilderness. His force was spotted by Union scouts at a couple different points of this journey, but Hooker and his staff dismissed their warnings of enemy movement as the products of overheated imaginations. Shortly before dusk, Jackson gave the order to attack. His assault bashed in the side of Hooker's army and forced the Federals into panicked retreat.

Nightfall brought a temporary end to the fighting between the two armies, but not to the bloodshed. While riding back to camp from a brief scouting excursion, Stonewall Jackson was shot by a group of his own soldiers, who mistook him for an enemy cavalryman. He died of his wounds a few days later, to the great distress of soldiers and civilians all across the Confederacy.

## Lee's Greatest Triumph

Despite Jackson's heroics the previous day, the outcome of the Battle of Chancellorsville remained in doubt when the sun came up on May 3. As the fighting resumed, however, Lee and top lieutenants like cavalry commander J. E. B. Stuart seemed to be one strategic step ahead of their Union counterparts at every turn. Rebel momentum grew with each passing hour, and the Union forces finally broke and fled the field. "The Bluecoats receded at last and thousands of powder-smeared Confederates poured into the clearing [at Chancellorsville], illuminated by flames from the burning Chancellorsville mansion," according to one historical account. "Lee emerged from the smoke and elicited along, unbroken cheer from the gray multitudes who recognized him as the architect of their improbable victory."[10]

By May 6 Hooker had completely retreated from the area. The Battle of Chancellorsville had cost him about 17,000 dead and wounded soldiers, about 15 percent of his total force. Lee's Army of Northern Virginia, meanwhile, had suffered 13,000 casualties, approximately 22 percent of its troop total, despite having a much smaller military force.

Lee's triumph at Chancellorsville convinced his troops that the general was virtually unbeatable in battle.

In the days following his remarkable victory, Lee's reputation as the conflict's most brilliant general seemed more secure than ever. "With little more than half as many men as [the] enemy," wrote scholar James M. McPherson, "Lee had grasped the initiative, gone over to the attack, and had repeatedly divided and maneuvered his forces in such a way as to give them superiority or equality of numbers at the point of attack. Like a rabbit mesmerized by the gray fox, Hooker was frozen into immobility and did not use half his power at any time in the battle."[11]

As great a triumph as Chancellorsville was for Lee, however, it also contained seeds of ruin for the commander and his beloved Army of Northern Virginia. "The boost that the battle gave to southern morale proved in the end harmful, for it bred an overconfidence in their own prowess and a contempt for the enemy that led to disaster," explained McPherson. "Believing his troops invincible, Lee was about to ask them to do the impossible."[12]

## Dreams of Striking a Decisive Blow

In mid-May Lee approached Confederate president Jefferson Davis and his closest advisors with a scheme to invade the North. The plan was exceedingly risky. The South's smaller armies and more limited military resources gave it less margin for error than the North. If Lee's Army of Northern Virginia suffered even one military setback of the scale that the Army of the Potomac had repeatedly absorbed in the war's first two years, the South's quest for independence from the United States might fall apart.

Nonetheless, Davis and his cabinet approved the plan. They were swayed in part by their faith in Lee and his seemingly magical military touch, but they were also intrigued by the many potential benefits of invasion. A successful push into the North could trigger a surge of antiwar sentiment in potential targets like Washington, Philadelphia, Baltimore, and Harrisburg, the state capital of Pennsylvania. If such antiwar feeling became strong enough, Lincoln would have to suspend military operations and accept that the Confederate states were irretrievable. A successful invasion of the North would also give war-weary Virginians a break—and it could even force the Union to call back troops from the West, which would greatly benefit battered Confederate armies and cities in that theatre. In addition, Lee pointed out that the rich farmlands of Pennsylvania and Maryland would give him ample opportunity to feed and resupply his troops. Instead of pulling from the South's fast-diminishing reserves, the Army

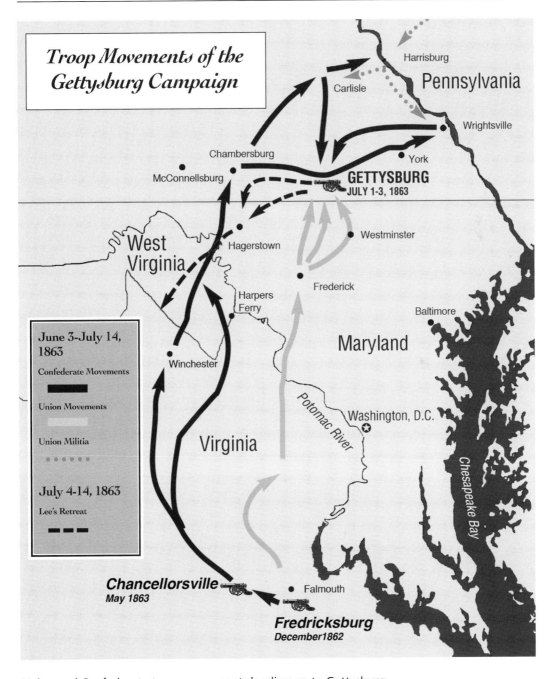

**Troop Movements of the Gettysburg Campaign**

Harrisburg

Pennsylvania

Carlisle

Wrightsville

Chambersburg

York

McConnellsburg

**GETTYSBURG**
JULY 1-3, 1863

West Virginia

Hagerstown

Westminster

Harpers Ferry

Frederick

Baltimore

**June 3-July 14, 1863**

Confederate Movements

Union Movements

Union Militia

**July 4-14, 1863**

Lee's Retreat

Maryland

Winchester

Potomac River

Washington, D.C.

Virginia

Chesapeake Bay

**Chancellorsville**
*May 1863*

Falmouth

**Fredricksburg**
*December1862*

Union and Confederate troop movements leading up to Gettysburg.

of Northern Virginia would be able to sustain itself on the crops, livestock, and other supplies of the enemy.

Finally, Lee emphasized that a successful sweep into the North might convince France and England to formally recognize the Confederate States of America as a legitimate nation. Such recognition would greatly intensify pressure on Lincoln to end the war and accept the departure of the slaveholding South from the United States. "Everything added up to the desirability of taking the calculated risk of a full-scale invasion," summarized military historian Edward J. Stackpole. "The Southern papers rejoiced audibly over the coming shift to the offensive. No apparent effort was made to keep the campaign a secret, possibly because the high command was so supremely confident of success.... [Confederate] newspapers advertised the forthcoming invasion weeks in advance, boasting of the manner in which they would fatten on the spoils to be taken from the prosperous farmers and full storehouses of the North."[13]

## Lee Crosses the Potomac

Lee's preparations for the march northward included a major reorganization of the Army of Northern Virginia. Prior to Jackson's death, the army had been divided into two corps. One had been under the command of Stonewall, while the other was helmed by Lieutenant General James Longstreet, who Lee fondly called his "old war horse" (see Longstreet biography, p. 148). Lee had come to feel, though, that Jackson's corps was too big for any potential successors to effectively manage. As tragic as Jackson's death at Chancellorsville had been for the South, his demise gave Lee an opportunity to re-form the army into three corps. Longstreet remained at the head of I Corps, Lieutenant General Richard S. Ewell took Jackson's spot as commander of II Corps, and Lieutenant General Ambrose Powell (A. P.) Hill was promoted to lead the newly minted III Corps [throughout this volume, specific Confederate corps are identified by Roman numeral (I, II, etc.) and Union corps are identified by Arabic numeral (1, 2, 3, etc.)]. These three infantry units were supplemented with a strong cavalry division led by the dashing J. E. B. "Jeb" Stuart (see Stuart biography, p. 16).

On June 3, Lee's army uncoiled from its camps surrounding Fredericksburg and began the long trek to the north. The force initially set a heading for the Shenandoah Valley, a fertile region of Virginia and West Virginia that provided a natural gateway into Pennsylvania. Over the next three weeks the Army of Northern Virginia moved steadily forward with Stuart's cavalry division in

The June 9 Battle of Brandy Station marked the first time that Union cavalry matched the skill and grit of the Confederate horsemen.

the lead, acting as a screen to keep Union eyes from discovering the full scale of the campaign. During this time Lee effortlessly rolled over token resistance from small Federal garrisons. On June 14-15, for example, Ewell's II Corps captured two small Union forts at Winchester, Virginia, in the Second Battle of Winchester. With this garrison muzzled, Ewell was able to easily transport his army across the Potomac River and into western Maryland. The rest of the Army of Northern Virginia followed on June 24-25.

Hooker's Army of the Potomac shadowed Lee and his invading army during much of this time, charting a parallel northward course to the east. For the most part he avoided contact with the enemy, focusing instead on keeping his columns between Lee and the big population centers of the North. The most notable exception to this cautious strategy, though, resulted in the largest cavalry battle that has ever been fought in North America.

The battle took place on June 9 at Brandy Station, Virginia, about 35 miles northwest of Fredericksburg, when 11,000 Union cavalrymen and infantry under the command of General Alfred Pleasonton launched a surprise pre-dawn attack against Stuart's encampment of 9,500 riders. Prior to this epic clash, Confederate cavalry forces had repeatedly embarrassed their Union counterparts. By the time of the Brandy Station showdown, the Southern horseman's superiority was unquestioned by either side. At Brandy Station, however, the Federal cavalry and its commanders, most notably John Buford and David McMurtrie Gregg, fought with such skill and determination against the much-celebrated Stuart that this stereotype was shredded. Although the day-long clash essentially ended in a draw and the Rebels managed to defend their position at Brandy Station, one of Stuart's top aides later admitted that the Battle of Brandy Station "made the Federal Cavalry.... The fact is that up to June 9, 1863, the Confederate cavalry did have its own way ... and the record of their success becomes almost monotonous.... But after that time we held our ground only by hard fighting."[14] Civil war historians have offered similar assessments of the battle's significance. "Brandy Station was no accident," wrote Stackpole. "The northern cavalry had at last come into its own! ... The day of easy Confederate triumphs was gone, never to return."[15]

## A Rebel Army in Pennsylvania

By late June all of Lee's Army of Northern Virginia had passed through Maryland and entered Pennsylvania's Cumberland Valley. Ewell's forces, in fact, had penetrated eastward to within twenty miles of the state capital of Harrisburg, sweeping through the small town of Gettysburg on their way. Most of the rest of Lee's army had settled in at Chambersburg, about twenty-five miles northwest of Gettysburg (See "The Army of Northern Virginia Invades Pennsylvania," p. 167). From here Confederate troops roamed the surrounding settlements and fields, taking food, clothing, horses, and other materials as they pleased. They even seized a few dozen African Americans—only a few of whom were fugitive slaves, the rest being legally free—and sent them South to enslavement under armed guard.

The looting and vandalism alarmed and outraged Northerners. However, it struck many Southern troops as perfectly justified, considering how Yankees had plundered the homes, shops, and fields of Virginians over the previous two years. When one woman in Pennsylvania personally complained to Longstreet about the loss of all her livestock to his men, the general defended their conduct by saying, "Yes, madam, it's very sad—very sad; and this sort of thing has been going on in Virginia more than two years—very sad."[16]

62

Meanwhile, Lee approved a request from Stuart to take three brigades of cavalry and head east over the Blue Ridge Mountains. Stuart was keenly aware that his being taken by surprise at Brandy Station had damaged his reputation. He believed that he could put that unpleasantness behind him with a foray into enemy territory, where he could conduct raids against Northern communities and frustrate the approaching Army of the Potomac with distracting strikes. Lee agreed to the scheme—provided that Stuart stayed in contact with the main army via courier and did not stray so far that he could not quickly return to the side of Lee or Ewell.

Lee's decision to allow cavalry commander J. E. B. Stuart to leave on an extended scouting mission had lasting repercussions.

Stuart and his three best brigades set out on the morning of June 25. Within a few days, though, the cavalry detachment found its path back to the rest of the Army of Northern Virginia cut off by the Army of the Potomac, which moved northward more quickly than Stuart or Lee anticipated. On June 28 Lincoln had removed Hooker from leadership of the Union force, replacing him with Major General George Gordon Meade (see Meade biography, p. 153). Upon taking over, Meade ordered his troops to pick up the pace of their pursuit of the Southern invaders. By the evening of June 29 the Army of the Potomac had advanced twenty-five miles northward and bolstered its positions along a twenty-mile swath that extended from the southern Pennsylvania border to Westminster, about twenty miles southwest of Gettysburg.

Unable to burst through the Northern ranks to reunite with Lee, Stuart was forced to push steadily northward until he could get ahead of Meade's forces, turn west, and find his fellow Confederates. He was not able to complete this task until July 2—by which time the famous Battle of Gettysburg was already in its second day. In other words, in the week leading up to the most pivotal clash of the entire Civil War, "the cavalry chief—upon whom [Lee] relied for information about enemy movements—might just as well have been on another planet."[17]

On the night of June 28 Lee received word from a civilian spy that Meade's Army of the Potomac was moving north out of Maryland and into Pennsylvania in apparent pursuit of the Army of Northern Virginia. A clash between the two great armies seemed increasingly inevitable. Lee expressed heightened frustration at the continued lack of information from Stuart about the exact size and specific route of the Union force. Nonetheless, Lee told one of his top aides that when he confronted the Army of the Potomac, he intended to "throw an overwhelming force on their advance, crush it, follow up the success, drive one corps back on another, and by successive repulses and surprises create a panic and virtually destroy the army.... If God gives us the victory, the war will be over and we shall achieve the recognition of our independence."[18]

## Notes

[1] Quoted in Hoke, Jacob. *The Great Invasion of 1863: Or, General Lee in Pennsylvania.* Dayton, OH: W. J. Shuey, 1887, p. 95.

[2] Quoted in McPherson, James M. *Hallowed Ground: A Walk at Gettysburg.* New York: Crown, 2003, p. 27.

[3] Quoted in Groom, Winston. *Vicksburg, 1863.* New York: Knopf, 2009, p. 421.

[4] Quoted in Winschel, Terrence J. *Triumph and Defeat: The Vicksburg Campaign.* New York: Savas Beatie, 2006, p. 74.

[5] "Siege of Vicksburg (May 26-July 3)," National Park Service, Vicksburg National Military Park, n.d. Retrieved from http://www.nps.gov/vick/historyculture/siege.htm.

[6] Quoted in Hoehling, Adolph A. *Vicksburg: 47 Days of Siege.* Mechanicsburg, PA: Stackpole Books, 1969, p. 116.

[7] Quoted in Shea, William L., and Terrence J. Winschel. *Vicksburg Is the Key: The Struggle for the Mississippi River.* Lincoln: University of Nebraska Press, 2003, p. 173.

[8] Quoted in Sears, Stephen W. *Chancellorsville.* New York: Houghton Mifflin, 1996, p. 120.

[9] Quoted in Green, A. Wilson. "Battle of Chancellorsville," National Park Service: Fredericksburg & Spotsylvania Military Park, n.d. Retrieved from http://www.nps.gov/frsp/chist.htm.

[10] Green, "Battle of Chancellorsville."

[11] McPherson, James M. *Battle Cry of Freedom: The Civil War Era.* New York: Oxford University Press, 1988, p. 646.

[12] McPherson, *Battle Cry of Freedom,* p. 646.

[13] Stackpole, Edward J. *They Met at Gettysburg.* Harrisburg, PA: Stackpole Books, 1996, p. 3.

[14] McClellan, Henry, quoted in Wittenberg, Eric J. *The Battle of Brandy Station: North America's Largest Cavalry Battle.* Charleston, SC: History Press, 2010, p. 190.

[15] Stackpole, p. 10.

[16] Quoted in McPherson, *Battle Cry of Freedom,* p. 649; from Lord, Walter, ed. *The Fremantle Diary: Being the Journal of Lieutenant Colonel James Arthur Lyon Fremantle, Coldstream Guards, on his Three Months in the Southern States.* Boston: 1954, p. 224.

[17] Editors of Time-Life. *Gettysburg: The Confederate High Tide* [Time-Life Civil War series]. Chicago: Time-Life Books, 1985, p. 28.

[18] Quoted in Foote, Shelby. *The Civil War: A Narrative, Volume Two: Fredericksburg to Meridian.* New York: Random House, 1963, p. 446.

# Chapter Four

# THE BATTLE IS JOINED

The hoarse and indistinguishable orders of commanding officers, the screaming and bursting of shells, canister and shrap-
nel as they tore through the struggling masses of humanity, the
death screams of wounded animals, the groans of their human
companions, wounded and dying and trampled underfoot by
hurrying batteries, riderless horses and the moving lines of battle—a perfect Hell on earth, never, perhaps to be equaled, certainly not to be surpassed, nor ever to be forgotten in a man's
lifetime. It has never been effaced from my memory, day or
night, for fifty years.[1]

—U.S. private William Archibald Waugh,
describing the Battle of Gettysburg

When General Robert E. Lee learned that the U.S. Army of the
Potomac was pushing northward into Pennsylvania to guard Washington, D.C., and other great cities of the North against Lee's
Army of Northern Virginia, he sensed an opportunity. Lee consulted with his
most trusted corps commander, General James Longstreet. The two men
agreed that the Army of the Potomac's freshly promoted leader, General
George Meade, was likely to proceed with great caution. They knew that it
would take Meade some time to organize his staff, and that he would feel great
pressure to avoid the humiliating defeats that had befallen Ambrose Burnside
and Joseph Hooker, his predecessors. If the Rebels found Meade's army and
struck swiftly and decisively, they might even be able to crush it so badly that
President Lincoln and the North would finally admit defeat and let the Confederacy go.

> *Union cavalry commander John Buford sensed that the gray soldiers in his field glasses were but the leading edge of a great wave of Confederate soldiers. The sight chilled him.*

On the evening of June 28 Lee told Longstreet that he intended to turn to meet the approaching enemy. The following morning, the two corps with Lee at Chambersburg—Longstreet's I Corps and Ambrose Powell (A. P.) Hill's III Corps—began moving east on Cashtown Road. A courier also was dispatched to the northeast to find Lieutenant General Richard S. Ewell and his II Corps, which were camped near the Pennsylvania state capital of Harrisburg. The courier carried orders from Lee for Ewell to suspend his operations there and turn his army back to the south. Ewell was told to meet up with the rest of the Army of Northern Virginia at a quaint little town called Gettysburg, where many of the region's main roads met (see "Lee's Army Advances to Gettysburg," p. 170).

In the meantime, Meade continued to move his army northward. His destination was Gettysburg as well, for the simple reason that the roads that the Union army was taking converged there too. Meade did not initially know that Lee and his Rebel army had turned about to meet him. On the morning of June 30, however, the leading edge of his army—Union cavalry under the command of John Buford, one of the heroes of Brandy Station—entered the outskirts of Gettysburg from the south. Almost immediately, Buford spotted an advance force of Confederate infantry approaching the town from the northeast. The sight chilled Buford, who sensed that the gray soldiers in his field glasses (binoculars) were but the leading edge of a great wave of Confederate soldiers over the horizon.

## Claiming the High Ground

When the Confederate force saw Buford's cavalry, it halted, then slowly withdrew back up Cashtown Road. The commander of this Rebel brigade, General J. Johnston Pettigrew, knew that the presence of Union cavalry likely meant that a large force of Yankee infantry also was in the vicinity. When Pettigrew reported back to Hill about the Union cavalry in Gettysburg, however, Hill decided that Pettigrew had only seen a detachment of Yankee infantry or state militia.

Lee accepted Hill's judgment, but the episode underscored just how much the Army of Northern Virginia missed J. E. B. Stuart's cavalry. Lee had received no updates from Stuart's scouts about enemy movements since June 28, when he had first learned of the approach of the Army of the Potomac. Angered and

66

bewildered by Stuart's continued absence, Lee nonetheless ordered the Army of Northern Virginia to keep marching toward Gettysburg.

In the meantime, back at Gettysburg, Buford sprang into action. First, he sent several advance cavalry scouts off into the hills to confirm his suspicion that the Army of Northern Virginia was headed for the town. He then surveyed the village and the surrounding countryside. He immediately took note of several high ridges and hills to the south of town that could be converted into strong defensive positions.

When Buford's scouts returned and told him that Lee was indeed coming their way, the cavalry officer made a bold decision. Convinced that whichever army took possession of Gettysburg's high ridges and hills would gain a huge battlefield advantage, Buford ordered his troops to prepare a line of defense on the northwest edge of town, straddling Cashtown Road, at a place

Union cavalry commander John Buford immediately recognized the importance of claiming the high ground at Gettysburg.

called McPherson's Ridge. He also sent an urgent message south to Major General John Reynolds, commander of the nearest corps of Union infantry. Buford's message informed Reynolds that a clash was imminent at Gettysburg, and that he urgently needed help.

Later that night Buford received a response. Reynolds urged Buford to stand his ground, and he promised to bring his corps as soon as possible the following morning. With this message in hand, Buford and his men waited anxiously as the night hours ticked by. If Reynolds arrived in time, the Federals would likely gain possession of the ridges and hills south of Gettysburg. If not, then Buford and his cavalry would be crushed, and the high ground would belong to Lee. Either way, Buford's decision to make a stand at Gettysburg paved the way for the quiet little town to become the site of one of the great battles of the American Civil War.

## The Battle Begins

Early the following morning—July 1—two brigades of Lee's Army of Northern Virginia came down Cashtown Road and within rifle range of Buford's

---

## The Myth of the Gettysburg Shoes

One of the enduring legends surrounding the Battle of Gettysburg is that the whole clash between Meade's Army of the Potomac and Lee's Army of Northern Virginia was triggered by the Confederates' desire to make off with shoes from a town shoe factory. In reality, however, no shoe factory existed in the town of Gettysburg, so there was no great supply of shoes available to be seized. "The Confederates were not coming to Gettysburg to get shoes," declared Gettysburg historian Tim Smith. "Ten roads intersect at the town, and both commanders had issued orders prior to the battle that would lead troops towards that intersection. Simply put, the battle was fought at Gettysburg because the roads led there."

### Source

"The First Day at Gettysburg: Then and Now. An Interview with Tim Smith." *Civil War Trust,* February 2011. Retrieved from http://www.civilwar.org/battlefields/gettysburg/gettysburg-2011/gettysburg-then-and-now.html.

---

men. The brigades were led by Major General Henry Heth of Virginia, who had served in the U.S. Army before the war, like many other Confederate officers.

At 7:30 a.m. the first shot of what came to be known as the Battle of Gettysburg was fired by a Union cavalry officer named Marcellus Jones of the Eighth Illinois Cavalry. As the gunfire from Buford's lines intensified, Heth's 7,500-man force set up its own lines on a ridge to the west of a creek called Willoughby's Run. Heth's troops probed forward, unsure of the strength of the force before them. Their early pushes were swatted down by Buford's troopers, who had spent the previous night building strong defenses for themselves. As time passed, however, the rest of Hill's corps came down the road and entered the fray.

Badly outnumbered and battered by intensifying Rebel artillery fire, Buford's valiant cavalry were on the verge of being overrun when Reynolds suddenly came galloping onto the scene. Close behind him were two of his best brigades, the famous Iron Brigade (which included regiments from Indiana, Michigan, and Wisconsin) and Pennsylvania's Bucktail Brigade. They were followed by the rest of Reynolds' force—the entirety of the Army of the Potomac's First Corps and portions of its Eleventh Corps.

This dramatic infusion of Union troops lifted the spirits of Buford and his men, and the fighting assumed an even fiercer pitch. As Reynolds was deploying his men, however, a Rebel bullet crashed into his skull and killed him. This was a severe blow to the Federals, for Reynolds was known to be one of the most talented officers in the entire Union army. As historian Noah Andre Trudeau wrote, "The death of John Reynolds meant more than the loss of an inspiring leader; it also removed from the equation the one person with enough vision and sense of purpose to manage this battle."[2]

By the early afternoon Confederate Lt. General Ewell's II Corps had arrived at Gettysburg from the north. Ewell ordered an assault on the enemy's right flank, which was manned by the Eleventh Corps under the command of Union Major General O. O. Howard. To the

The death of General John F. Reynolds on the first day of battle was a severe blow to the Union.

west, meanwhile, Hill increased the pressure on the Union's First Corps, which was now under the direction of Major General Abner Doubleday. Federal scouts rushed back to Meade to inform him that a good portion of his army was now engaged in a desperate struggle for survival against the Army of Northern Virginia. When Meade heard the news, he ordered the remainder of his army forward to Gettysburg. His force was so large, however, that progress was slow. Most of the Army of the Potomac would not be able to reach the battlefield before nightfall.

Meanwhile, Lee and Longstreet were riding together on Cashtown Road, still several miles from Gettysburg, when they heard the unmistakable sounds of heavy cannon fire in the distance. Alarmed, Lee told Longstreet to prepare his corps for battle, then rode ahead to see what was going on. "Lee galloped toward Gettysburg like a blinded giant," wrote historian Douglas Southall Freeman. "He did not know where the Federals were, or how numerous they might be. Ewell—and doubtless Hill also—had cautioned not to bring on a general engagement with a strong adversary until the rest of the infantry came up, but with no cavalry to inform him, he could not tell what calamity he might invite by advancing at all, or what opportunity he might lose by advancing cautiously. Never had he been so dangerously in the dark."[3]

## Chased Through Gettysburg

Once Lee arrived at the western outskirts of Gettysburg and received reports from Hill, Ewell, and their staffs, he immediately grasped the potential stakes of the escalating showdown. Both armies were throwing new troops into the battle with every hour (an estimated 30,000 Confederate and 18,000 Federal troops eventually participated in the first day's action), and casualties on both sides were quickly piling up. The confrontation had flared to life by accident, but it now had the potential to become one of the pivotal battles of the entire war. And although the Federal troops were fighting well, they badly missed Reynolds's leadership and tactical skills.

Sensing advantage, Lee watched approvingly as Hill's divisional commanders—Heth, William Dorsey Pender, and Robert E. Rodes—launched new offensives against the Union positions. As these barrages of rifle and artillery fire punished the Union's left flank, the Federals' right flank was hit by Major General Jubal Early and a division of Rebel troops. Early was in many respects the dominant officer of II Corps, even though Ewell was technically the corps' commanding officer. Early's assault succeeded in buckling the defenses of Howard's Eleventh Corps. The Rebels overran their position at about 4 p.m., setting off a disastrous chain reaction down the beleaguered Yankee line. As Confederate troops poured in from the north, the two-mile line of Union defenses caved in from right to left like a row of dominos. Within a matter of minutes, hundreds of Federal soldiers were fleeing south through the streets of Gettysburg (see "Impressions of the Battle from a British Observer," p. 173).

As the Union lines broke, Confederate troops gleefully gave chase, and for a brief time it appeared that Gettysburg was simply another Civil War clash that was going to end in a decisive victory for Lee and the Army of Northern Virginia. In reality, however, the soldiers in blue were not fleeing blindly. They had a destination in mind: the tops of Cemetery Hill and Culp's Hill, two high positions that overlooked the southern end of the village. Hours earlier, Howard had stationed a small division of troops and artillery atop Cemetery Hill. These soldiers had spent the afternoon digging trenches and making other preparations to withstand a Rebel assault, and their position became a refuge and rallying point for the Union troops who had been chased through town.

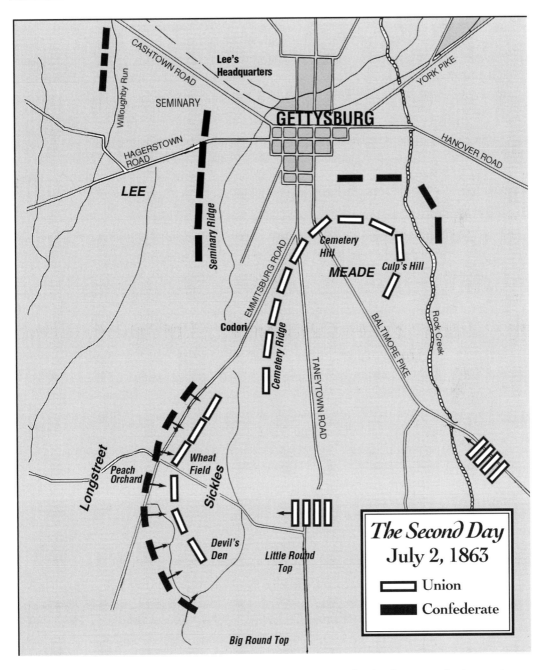

CASHTOWN ROAD

Lee's
Headquarters

Willoughby Run

SEMINARY

YORK PIKE

**GETTYSBURG**

HAGERSTOWN
ROAD

HANOVER ROAD

**LEE**

Seminary Ridge

EMMITSBURG ROAD

Cemetery
Hill

Culp's Hill

**MEADE**

Codori

Cemetery Ridge

Rock Creek

BALTIMORE PIKE

TANEYTOWN ROAD

Longstreet

Peach
Orchard

Wheat
Field

Sickles

Devil's
Den

Little Round
Top

*The Second Day*
**July 2, 1863**

Union

Confederate

Big Round Top

Confederate and Unions positions after Sickles made his unauthorized troop redeployments.

of each of these positions one by one, delivering horrible punishment to the enemy at each spot. Sickles was among the casualties, as his right leg was nearly severed by a Rebel cannonball. As he was carried off the field of battle, Sickles lit up a cigar in an effort to show his unconcern and shore up the spirits of his bloodied troops.

Union infantry and artillery took a fearsome toll on the Confederate forces as well. Valuable officers like Brigadier General William Barksdale (13th Mississippi), who led the charge that first punctured the Union defenses at the Peach Orchard, were slain in the offensive. Anonymous Rebel infantrymen fell by the hundreds as well, their lives snuffed out by withering barrages from Yankee bullets, cannonballs, explosive shells, and canister shot.

As the battle wore on it became increasingly unclear whether Longstreet had enough men to fully cave in the Union lines, which re-formed (with reinforcements from Meade) back at Cemetery Ridge. Again and again the Southerners came up the ridge, desperate to collapse the enemy's fraying line, but again and again the Northerners repulsed them.

## The Battle for Little Round Top

As the clash wore on, portions of Hood's division pushed to the western slopes of Little Round Top, which Sickles had left undefended with his move to the Peach Orchard. These Confederate troops included three regiments under the command of Brigadier General J. B. Robertson—the 4th Texas, 5th Texas, and 4th Alabama—and several regiments under Brigadier General E. M. Law, including the 15th Alabama and 47th Alabama. Meade initially assumed that Sickles had at least had the sense to keep a defensive force entrenched at Little Round Top, which anchored the far left flank of the Union position. Around the time that the Law and Robertson brigades began weaving through the woods at the base of the hill, however, Meade sent an aide, Brigadier General Gouverneur K. Warren, to see if the Little Round Top defenses needed shoring up.

When Warren huffed up to the top of the hill, he was stunned to find it empty of Union troops except for a small squad of U.S. Signal Corps observers. Warren immediately sent his officers out in search of nearby troops to defend the strategically vital hill. This urgent request was received by Major General George Sykes, commander of the Union V Corps, who sent a redeployment order out to a division led by Brigadier General James Barnes. Sykes's messenger, though, first ran into Brigadier General Strong Vincent, commander of the

Artist's rendering of Union general Gouverneur K. Warren's ascent of Little Round Top, when he discovered that the hill was vulnerable to Confederate attack.

V Corps' Third Brigade. Vincent immediately grasped the perilous situation, and he hurriedly took four regiments to Little Round Top.

Vincent frantically arranged his four regiments—the 16th Michigan, the 44th New York, the 83rd Pennsylvania, and the 20th Maine—into a defensive semi-circle along the western slope of Little Round Top. This dispersal placed Colonel Joshua Lawrence Chamberlain and the 20th Maine at the far southern end (left flank) of the entire Union defense (see Chamberlain biography, p. 125). Vincent emphasized to Chamberlain that he and his men had to hold their position at all costs. If they were pushed aside, the Confederate attackers would have an open lane northward to attack the undefended backsides of the entire Army of the Potomac—as well as an ideal position from which to launch devastating artillery barrages.

Less than fifteen minutes after Vincent placed his 1,300 or so troops, Rebel infantry appeared out of the woods below. They charged forward with fierce determination, and a vicious battle ensued all across the western slope of Lit-

An artist's depiction of the Confederate charge up Little Round Top on July 2 at Gettysburg.

tle Round Top. When elements of the 4th and 5th Texas regiments crashed into the 16th Michigan, it appeared that they might break through. Vincent, however, rallied his forces with the help of the timely arrival of the 140th New York under Colonel Patrick O'Rorke. The Confederates were finally forced to withdraw back down the slope, though not before delivering mortal wounds to both Vincent and O'Rorke.

Hood's division also nearly broke through against Chamberlain and the 20th Maine, which the war had thinned to fewer than 400 men by Gettysburg. Soldiers of the 15th and 47th Alabama regiments, commanded by Colonel William C. Oates, came at Chamberlain's position in wave after wave. The 20th Maine barely repulsed each of these attacks. After an hour and a half, though, Chamberlain's regiment ran out of ammunition. As Oates's men came up through the woods once again, Chamberlain ordered a bayonet attack. This desperate strategy was more successful than Chamberlain could have dreamed. When the 20th Maine leaped out from behind their barricades and charged downhill, bayonets flashing, the Rebels were so stunned and disoriented that their entire offensive collapsed. They fled the hill in disarray, and Vincent's Fifth Corps collected hundreds of prisoners (see "Chamberlain Describes the Battle of Little Round Top," p. 178).

Chamberlain's daring gambit and the valiant performance of the other Fifth Corps regiments thus kept Little Round Top in Union hands. Meade later wrote that the successful defense of Little Round Top was a pivotal moment in the entire battle. "But for the timely advance of the Fifth Corps and the prompt sending of a portion to Round Top, where they met the enemy almost on the crest and had a desperate fight to secure the position—I say but for these circumstances the enemy would have secured Round Top, planted his artillery there, commanding the whole battlefield, and what the result would have been I leave you to judge."[9]

## Successful Defense of Culp's Hill and Cemetery Hill

By the early evening of July 2, the bloody engagements for control of the battlefield's southwestern precincts were drawing to a close. The exhausted Union and Confederate survivors of the Peach Orchard, Devil's Den, Little Round Top, and other clashes returned to their camps and lines, dragging wounded comrades and prisoners back with them. Up at Cemetery Hill and Culp's Hill, though, the bloodshed continued for several more hours.

Ewell's instructions for the day from Lee had called for him to maintain steady pressure on the Union's northern front—the curve of the fish hook—to prevent Meade and his commanders from sending Culp's Hill and Cemetery Hill defenders to the southern end of the Union defenses as reinforcements for Sickles. Lee also firmly instructed Ewell to launch a full-scale offensive if he thought that the Union positions he faced could be conquered.

In mid-afternoon Ewell's artillery began exchanging fire with the Union guns up on the heights, and hostilities continued to escalate between the two sides through the early evening. By the time dusk began to descend on Gettysburg, Confederate commanders had launched a number of probing attacks that nearly reached the crest of Culp's Hill and Cemetery Hill. Rebel forces under the direction of Major General Edward "Allegheny" Johnson even managed to seize control of trench works along the lower reaches of Culp's Hill.

That was as far as the Confederates got, however. Punishing artillery fire from Union guns, timely deployments of reinforcements by Hancock, and

Union forces under Winfield S. Hancock turned back repeated Confederate assaults on Culp's Hill and Cemetery Hill on Day Two.

heroic performances by several Federal regiments kept the hills in Meade's hands. On Culp's Hill, for example, the 137th New York (led by Colonel David Ireland) and four other New York regiments under the command of Brigadier General George S. Greene withstood a sustained nighttime offensive from a full division of Confederate infantry. "The 137th New York's stand [at the far right end of the Union defenses] was just as impressive and important as the defensive accomplishments of the 20th Maine a short time before at the other end of the Army of the Potomac's line,"[10] wrote military historian Jeffrey C. Hall.

## Two Bloodied but Unbowed Armies

The day's bloodshed finally ended late in the evening of July 2, though the night continued to be punctuated by occasional rifle shots from nervous sentries. Day two at Gettysburg had been one of the bloodiest of the entire war. Each army had suffered about 10,000 casualties during the course of the day. Only the one-day Battle of Antietam, which had resulted in the death or wounding of 23,000 soldiers, exceeded July 2 for carnage and devastation.

Nonetheless, Lee expressed confidence that the Army of Northern Virginia was on the verge of a great victory. His spirits were buoyed by the arrival that evening not only of Pickett's division, but also of Stuart's long-absent cavalry brigades, which had finally completed their long trek around the enemy's lines. Armed with these fresh assets, Lee decided that one more major offensive would break the Army of the Potomac once and for all.

Behind the Union lines at Meade's headquarters, though, confidence was also running high. General John Sedgwick's Sixth Corps had arrived, giving a big boost to the Federals' defensive lines. Meade sent a message to Washington informing Henry Halleck, the general-in-chief of the entire Union army, that "the enemy attacked me about 4 p.m. this day, and, after one of the severest contests of the war, was repulsed at all points. We have suffered considerably in

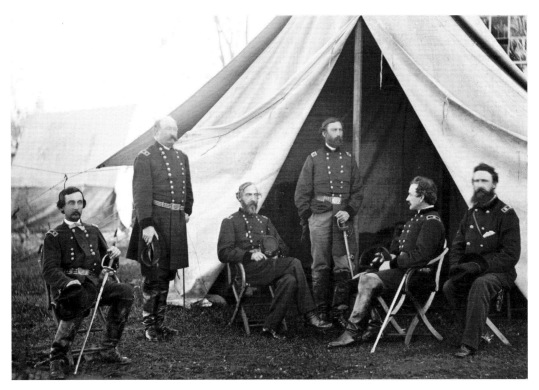

General George Meade and some of his officers two months after Gettysburg (Gouverneur K. Warren, William H. French, Meade, Henry J. Hunt, Andrew A. Humphreys, and George Sykes).

killed and wounded.... I shall remain in my present position tomorrow, but am not prepared to say, until better advised of the condition of the army, whether my operations will be of an offensive or defensive character."[11]

Later that evening, Meade called all his senior staff and battlefield commanders together for a war council in order to more fully assess "the condition of the army." Their reports, combined with their statements of support for staying and fighting, reassured Meade that the Army of the Potomac was ready if Lee decided to go another round (see "Meade Decides to Stay Put after Day Two at Gettysburg," p. 184). The atmosphere, according to one Wisconsin officer in attendance, was remarkably calm. The generals were as "mild-mannered and as free from flurry or excitement as a board of commissioners [meeting] to discuss a street improvement,"[12] he reported.

As the war council concluded, Meade turned to Major General John Gibbon, a North Carolina native who had three brothers fighting for the Confederacy. "If Lee attacks me tomorrow, it will be on *your front*," Meade reportedly told Gibbon, whose Second Corps division was stationed along the midsection of Cemetery Ridge. When Gibbon asked him why he thought so, Meade explained: "He has tried my left and failed, and has tried my right and failed; now, if he concludes to try it again, he will try the centre, right on your front."[13]

## Notes

[1]   Quoted in Carter, Robert Goldthwaite, ed. *Four Brothers in Blue: A Story of the Great Civil War from Bull Run to Appomattox.* 1913. Reprint ed. Norman: University of Oklahoma Press, 1999, p. 311.

[2]   Trudeau, Noah Andre. *Gettysburg: A Testing of Courage.* New York: HarperCollins, 2002, p. 271.

[3]   Freeman, Douglas Southall. *R. E. Lee: A Biography.* Vol. 3. New York: Scribner's, 1978, p. 68.

[4]   "Battle of Gettysburg: Confederate General Richard Ewell's Failure on the Heights," *HistoryNet.com,* June 12, 2006. Retrieved from http://www.historynet.com/battle-of-gettysburg-confederate-general-richard-ewells-failure-on-the-heights.htm.

[5]   McPherson, James M. *Hallowed Ground: A Walk at Gettysburg.* New York: Crown, 2003, p. 56.

[6]   Quoted in Foote, Shelby. *The Civil War: A Narrative. Volume Two: Fredericksburg to Meridian.* New York: Random House, 1963, p. 483.

[7]   Quoted in Pfanz, Harry W. *Gettysburg: The Second Day.* Chapel Hill: University of North Carolina Press, 1987, p. 26.

[8]   McPherson, pp. 69-70.

[9]   Meade, George Gordon. Letter to G. G. Benedict, March 16, 1870. In *Battles and Leaders of the Civil War,* Volume 3. Edited by Robert Underwood Johnson and Clarence Clough Buel. New York: Century Co., 1888, p. 414.

[10]  Hall, Jeffrey C. *The Stand of the U.S. Army at Gettysburg.* Bloomington: Indiana University Press, 2003, p. 153.

[11]  Quoted in Sears, Stephen W. *Gettysburg.* Boston: Houghton Mifflin, 2003, pp. 341-42.

[12]  Bryant, Edward Eustace. *History of the Third Regiment of Wisconsin Veteran Volunteer Infantry, 1861-1865.* Madison, WI: Veterans' Association of the Regiment, 1891, p. 191.

[13]  Meade, George Gordon. *The Life and Letters of George Gordon Meade.* Vol. 2. New York: Charles Scribner's Sons, 1913, p. 97.

# Chapter Five

# PICKETT'S CHARGE AND LEE'S RETREAT

◄───⟨∘⟩───►

Never was I so depressed as upon that [third day at Gettysburg]. I felt that my men were to be sacrificed, and that I should have to order them to make a hopeless charge.[1]

—Confederate lieutenant general James Longstreet

D uring the pre-dawn hours of July 3, soldiers in both Confederate general Robert E. Lee's Army of Northern Virginia and Union general George Meade's Army of the Potomac undoubtedly struggled mightily to sleep. Although they were emotionally and physically exhausted from the previous two days' fighting, their minds churned with the knowledge that the new day would likely bring another round of carnage and death for both sides.

The night was a restless one for the key commanders of the two armies as well. Meade and his top generals—Winfield Scott Hancock, Henry W. Slocum, O. O. Howard, David B. Birney, George Sykes, and John Sedgwick—felt confident of their position, but they knew from bitter experience that Lee was capable of snatching victory out of the jaws of defeat. Meanwhile, Lee and his "Old War Horse"—General James Longstreet—found themselves once again at odds over battle strategy.

## Lee and Longstreet Clash Again

During the evening of July 2 Lee had decided on a bold plan for the following morning: use Lieutenant General Richard S. Ewell's II Corps troops to once again attack the enemy's right side at Culp's Hill, then send a dagger straight into the center of the Federal lines in the form of 15,000 of Longstreet's I Corps troops. Lee believed that if the center offensive succeeded, he could break the spine of the enemy's line and send the Army of the Potomac fleeing from the field in humiliation, just as he had done at Chancellorsville a mere two months before. He sent out orders to Longstreet and the other generals informing them of the plan, then retired for the night.

Before sunrise the next morning, Lee rode out from his field headquarters on Seminary Ridge to see how Longstreet's preparations for the dawn assault were coming along. As soon as Lee pulled up, however, Longstreet greeted him by stating that "I have had my scouts out all night, and I find that you still have an excellent opportunity to move around to the right of Meade's army, and maneuver him into attacking us."[2] Lee testily rejected this advice, which Longstreet had already given on multiple occasions over the previous few days. "The enemy is there," Lee said, pointing at the heights of Cemetery Ridge, "and I am going to strike him."[3]

Longstreet listened despondently. Lee's offensive called for his men to advance on foot over nearly a mile of open ground to the Union line arrayed along Cemetery Ridge. Throughout this march they would be continuously exposed to heavy artillery and rifle fire. "General Lee," Longstreet finally said, according to his own memoirs. "I have been a soldier all my life. I have been with soldiers engaged in fights by couples, by squads, companies, regiments, divisions, and armies, and should know as well as anyone what soldiers can do. It is my opinion that no fifteen thousand men ever arrayed for battle can take that position."[4] His pleas to reconsider were turned aside by Lee, however, and Longstreet sorrowfully began preparing his corps for the attack. Major General George Pickett's division, which had arrived at Gettysburg the night before, was selected to spearhead the offensive. Pickett's division would be further supplemented by six brigades borrowed from A. P. Hill's III Corps under the direction of Brigadier General J. Johnston Pettigrew and Major General Isaac R. Trimble.

## A Third Day of Battle Begins

By the time Longstreet and Lee had their tense exchange, combatants in the northern reaches of the battlefield had already resumed their efforts to destroy one another. This clash at Culp's Hill between Ewell's II Corps and a division of the Union's Twelfth Corps commanded by Major General John White Geary began about 4:30 a.m., when Federal artillery unexpectedly opened up against Rebel troops that had captured trenches on the lower slopes of the hill the night before.

Ewell responded to the Union barrage with his own artillery, as well as a series of infantry charges meant to throw the Yankees off the hill once and for

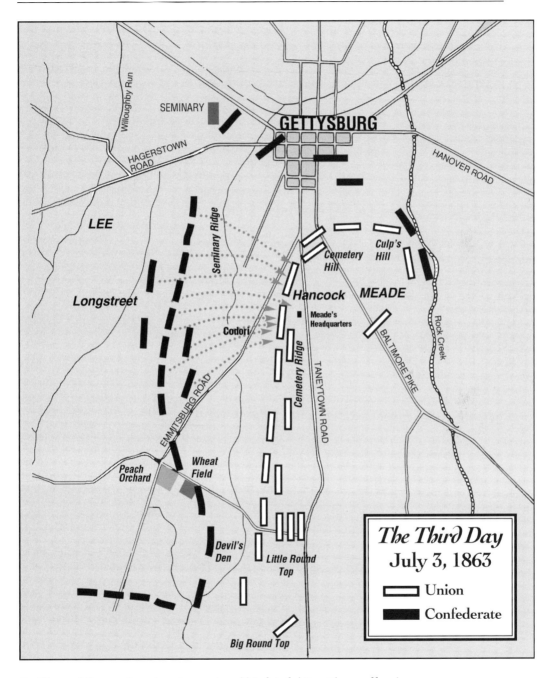

The Third Day
July 3, 1863

☐ Union

■ Confederate

Positions of the armies when Lee ordered his fateful Day Three offensive.

all. Hours of brutal fighting ensued on the high slopes of Culp's Hill, but the rebels were never able to break through. Their failure stemmed in large part from the unyielding performance of units such as the five New York regiments of Brigadier General George S. Greene, which had already proved their mettle in combat the previous day. Around 11:00 a.m. Ewell's forces withdrew a final time.

> *"So sudden and violent was the collision [between the two cavalries] that many of the horses were turned end over end and crushed their riders beneath them," recalled one Union cavalryman.*

"Ewell's corps … would do no more fighting at Gettysburg," observed one battle history. "For decades thereafter on Culp's Hill a ghostly forest would stand, its trees shorn of their limbs and stripped of their bark by flying metal—testimony to the savagery of a contest that would nevertheless be overshadowed by events still to come."[5]

A short time after the guns at Culp's Hill fell silent, another noteworthy clash erupted. This one took place between the armies' two cavalries. The Confederates' cavalry commander, Major General Jeb Stuart, knew that his absence over the previous several days had hindered Lee's military operations, so he was eager to make amends. On the morning of July 3, Stuart was instructed by Lee to take his four brigades—roughly 6,000 horsemen—and circle eastward below the Union position. He would then move north for the purpose of disrupting enemy communications and distracting the defenders of Cemetery Ridge, where Lee planned to focus the day's assault.

Stuart rode out into the countryside and traveled down along the Union's eastern flank without incident. Upon reaching an open plain about three miles south of Gettysburg, however, Stuart was confronted by about 4,500 Union cavalry commanded by Brigadier General David McMurtrie Gregg. The two forces collided about 1:00 p.m., and for the next two hours, large bands of warring horsemen and dismounted cavalry trampled back and forth across the rolling plain, which came to be known as East Cavalry Field. The ranks of both cavalries steadily thinned as bullets, artillery, sabers, and bone-breaking spills from horseback all took their toll.

Participants on both sides marveled at the skill and bravery the Rebel and Federal horsemen displayed throughout this clash. One Union cavalry captain from Pennsylvania recalled a particularly memorable episode during the battle. At one point a brigade of South Carolina riders under Brigadier General Wade Hampton were challenged head-on by the First Michigan, a cavalry brigade led by Brigadier General George Armstrong Custer (who in 1876

The carnage on the third day of battle began at Culp's Hill, where Lee's forces launched a series of morning assaults.

would secure a more prominent place in America's history books by leading 263 U.S. soldiers to their deaths at the hands of Cheyenne and Lakota Sioux Indians at the Battle of Little Bighorn in Montana). "As the two columns approached each other the pace of each increased, when suddenly a crash, like the falling of timber, betokened the crisis," wrote the Pennsylvanian. "So sudden and violent was the collision that many of the horses were turned end over end and crushed their riders beneath them. The clashing of sabers, the firing of pistols, the demands for surrender and cries of the combatants … filled the air."[6]

By mid-afternoon, steady pressure from Federal artillery and flanking attacks by Gregg's troops forced Stuart to suspend his efforts to attack the enemy's rear. He reluctantly ordered a retreat, and the epic clash of cavalry drew to a close. Neither side could claim a clear-cut victory. Stuart's forces suffered at least 181 casualties, with one brigade failing to report their killed, wounded, or captured, while

Gregg reported a loss of 254 men. Nonetheless, historians have credited Gregg and his horsemen with neutralizing a threat that might otherwise have distracted Meade, Hancock, and the other Union commanders from the main battle that unfolded that same afternoon at Cemetery Ridge.

## Softening Up the Union Defenses

Before Lee launched his central July 3 offensive against Meade's defenses arrayed along Cemetery Ridge, he ordered an extended barrage from Confederate cannons. These Rebel cannonballs and shells were designed to "soften up" the point of attack for the coming offensive—a stand of Yankee-filled woods perched midway along the ridge. The Union's artillery units responded in kind, and for the next two hours the hills south of Gettysburg echoed with the roar of the big guns.

Gradually, however, many of the Union's artillery batteries shut down one-by-one under orders from Meade's chief of artillery, Brigadier General Henry J. Hunt. Hunt's sly tactic not only enabled him to conserve ammunition for the infantry attack that he sensed was coming, it also fooled the Confederates into thinking that many of his cannons had been knocked out of action. The thick clouds of gun smoke that billowed over the field gave the Confederates no way to tell that, in reality, most of their cannonade fell harmlessly a short distance behind the Union lines.

As the Union guns fell silent, the Confederate cannons followed suit. "A deathlike stillness then reigned over the field," wrote Confederate brigadier general A. L. Long, "and each army remained in breathless expectation of something yet to come still more dreadful."[7] At about 3:00 p.m. Pickett received a note from the Confederate artillery chief, Colonel Edward Porter Alexander. The note informed him that most of the Union guns had been "driven off," and that the time had come to initiate Lee's assault on Cemetery Ridge. Pickett immediately rode over to Longstreet and asked for permission to advance. Overwhelmed by emotion, Longstreet could not bring himself to speak. Instead, he grimly nodded his head. Pickett wheeled away in excitement, thrilled that his division would finally have a chance to make its mark at Gettysburg.

## Pickett's Charge

Pickett pulled up in front of his division and his brigade commanders—James L. Kemper, Richard B. Garnett, and Lewis A. Armistead (whose best friend before the war had been Hancock, the general now commanding the Union defenses at Cemetery Ridge). "Up men, and to your posts! Don't forget today that you are from old Virginia!" he trumpeted loudly, then gave the order to advance. Pickett's division marched eastward out of the woods and onto the open field that separated the Confederate encampments at Seminary Ridge from the Union defenses atop Cemetery Ridge. As they moved forward, Pickett's troops linked up with the brigades commanded by Pettigrew and Trimble, which were also emerging from cover. The total number of Rebel troops involved in Pickett's Charge, as the offensive came to be known, ran to about 12,000—3,000 less than Longstreet and Lee originally thought they had at their disposal.

Federal officers atop Cemetery Ridge instructed their troops, most of whom were well-protected behind a low stone wall, to hold their fire until the enemy was within range. They did not have long to wait. As the Confederate charge gathered steam and poured over Emmitsburg Road toward the slopes of the Union-held ridge, Hunt's artillery batteries and infantry commanded by Major General John Gibbon and Brigadier General Alexander Hays dealt out terrible punishment to the brave Rebels at the front of the charge (see "A Rebel Officer Remembers Pickett's Charge," p. 186). Shells and bullets scorched the flanks of the Confederates as well from as far away as Little Round Top and Cemetery Hill.

The whole scene was a torment to Longstreet, who watched helplessly as "the slaughter he had predicted" came true, in the words of Civil War historian Jeffrey Wert. "Union cannon crews and infantrymen blasted apart the Southern units in a gale of death."[8]

The battle-weary brigades led by Trimble and Pettigrew were the first to falter under the heavy hail of enemy fire, though the tattered remains of the 26th North Carolina fought their way to within a dozen yards of the Union line before being vanquished. Pickett's fresh brigades pressed up the slopes in greater number, and 100 or more Virginians led by Armistead actually managed to breach the stone wall at the crest of Cemetery Ridge, at a place that would come to be known as the Bloody Angle.

General George Pickett was excited at the prospect of leading the Confederates' Day Three assault on Cemetery Ridge.

91

An engraving of Pickett's Charge against the Union forces atop Cemetery Ridge.

For a few brief moments Armistead and his men gloried in the knowledge that they had pierced the enemy's defensive line and "planted their colors." Years later, in fact, this attainment of the heights of Cemetery Ridge would come to be known as the High Water Mark of the rebellion. But Federal reinforcements from the 19th Massachusetts, 42nd New York, and 72nd Pennsylvania quickly poured in to assist the beleaguered 69th Pennsylvania and fill this small rupture in the Union line. One participant in this desperate clash remembered that the two enemy lines crashed together with a "shock":

> The opposing lines were standing as if rooted, dealing death into each other…. Foot to foot, body to body, and man to man they struggled, pushed and strived and killed. The mass of wounded and heaps of dead entangled the feet of the contestants, and, underneath the trampling mass, wounded men who could no longer stand, struggled, fought, shouted and killed—hatless,

coatless, drowned in sweat, black with powder, red with blood, with fiendish yells and strange oaths they blindly plied the work of slaughter.[9]

Within a matter of minutes, the Confederates were overwhelmed by the enemy's superior numbers. Armistead was captured after being wounded (he died two days later), and the rest of the Rebel invaders of the ridge were killed, captured, or driven away (see "A Yankee Soldier Recalls Pickett's Charge," p. 190).

The confrontation at the Bloody Angle marked the end of Pickett's Charge (sometimes termed the Pickett-Pettigrew Charge by historians). The great gray wave that had spilled across the fields below Cemetery Ridge and lapped the base of the Union's stone walls had spent itself. The remnants of that wave now receded, leaving behind a shocking tableau of torn and bloodied bodies. No formal call of retreat was ever issued by Pickett or other commanders, but a sort of unspoken understanding rippled through the Confederate ranks. Those who had thus far survived the assault turned quietly and limped back to Lee and Longstreet, mostly silent but for the groans of pain from wounds suffered in battle. As they returned to their encampment several Rebels passed by Lee himself, who seemed shattered by the turn of events. "All this has been my fault," he reportedly said to a number of soldiers.

## The Deadly Toll

Pickett's Charge resulted in an estimated 1,500 Union casualties, about 20 percent of the total number of blue-clad soldiers that saw action on and around Cemetery Ridge that day. The damage to Lee's army, though, was much more extensive. More than half of the 12,000 or so Confederate troops that participated in the charge were slain, wounded, or captured during the hour-long offensive.

Pickett escaped the carnage without injury, but many other top officers were wounded or killed in the action. "Trimble went down with a wound that would cost him a leg," wrote McPherson. "Pettigrew received a flesh wound in the hand. Garnett's riderless horse bolted out of the smoke; his master's body was later buried with his men and never identified. Kemper was crippled by a severe wound. All fifteen regimental commanders in Pickett's division went down; nine of them were killed. Thirteen of Pickett's regiments suffered the ignominy of having their flags captured by the enemy."[10]

Pickett himself was enormously proud of his men, though he gave great credit to the Union force at Cemetery Ridge for turning back the Confederate

Confederate dead on the battlefield at Gettysburg.

charge. Years later, Pickett's widow reported that when her husband was asked why the charge failed, he responded, "I've always thought the Yankees had something to do with it."[11] In the immediate aftermath of the offensive, though, Pickett's primary emotion was sorrow—perhaps tinged with anger at what Lee's orders had wrought. Observers reported that when Lee rode up to him and instructed him to reorganize his divisions in the event that the Yankees counterattacked, a tearful Pickett replied, "General Lee, I have no division now."[12]

## Lee's Retreats and Meade's Cautious Pursuit

Pickett's Charge marked the last significant clash of the Battle of Gettysburg. Lee had lost more than one-third of his army at Gettysburg, having

## Surveying the Wreckage of War

As General Robert E. Lee and the Army of Northern Virginia departed Gettysburg, Union burial parties began to drift out onto the now-silent battlefield. They were joined by Yankee survivors who felt drawn to the scene. One such survivor was Sergeant Thomas D. Marbaker of the 11th New Jersey, who later wrote about what he saw:

> Upon the open fields [of Gettysburg], like sheaves bound by the reaper, in crevices of the rocks, behind fences, trees and buildings; in thickets, where they had crept for safety only to die in agony; by stream or wall or hedge, wherever the battle had raged or their weakening steps could carry them, lay the dead. Some, with faces bloated and blackened beyond recognition, lay with glassy eyes staring up at the blazing summer sun; others, with faces downward and clenched hands filled with grass or earth, which told of the agony of [their] last moments. Here a headless trunk, there a severed limb; in all the grotesque positions that unbearable pain and intense suffering contorts the human form, they lay....

> All around was the wreck the battlestorm leaves in its wake—broken caissons [ammunition carts], dismounted guns, small arms bent and twisted by the storm or dropped and scattered by disabled hands; dead and bloated horses, torn and ragged equipment, and all the sorrowful wreck that the waves of battle leave at their ebb; and over all, hugging the earth like a fog, poisoning every breath, the pestilential stench of decaying humanity.

### Source

Marbaker, Thomas D. *History of the Eleventh New Jersey Volunteers: From Its Organization to Appomattox.* Trenton, NJ: MacCrellish and Quigley, 1898.

incurred approximately 28,000 casualties over three days. The Army of Northern Virginia's stores of ammunition and other supplies had also reached dangerously low levels. Lee thus quietly gathered together his crippled force and prepared to withdraw from the scene. He sent messengers to Meade offering a

President Lincoln expressed deep anger when he learned that Lee had escaped back into Virginia.

prisoner exchange, but his suggestion was rebuffed by the Union chief. Unfazed, Lee made sure that he had adequate transport arrangements for his many wounded men and about 4,000 prisoners. Lee gave the order for the Army of Northern Virginia to begin their departure late on July 4. His battered and disappointed army set out for home—Virginia—in a driving rain as Union observers watched impassively.

The Army of Northern Virginia soon passed out of Pennsylvania and into Maryland, but their progress was halted in Williamsport, at the rain-swollen edge of the Potomac River. Lee and his men spent the next week there, cobbling together bridges, waiting for the waters to recede, and warding off harassing attacks from Union cavalry. Each day the Rebels feared a full-scale attack from Meade, but it never came, despite furious prodding from General-in-Chief Henry Halleck and President Lincoln himself (see "General Lee Writes Home after Gettysburg," p. 196). Instead, the Army of the Potomac followed at a distance, mostly content to let its cavalry buzz around Lee like angry hornets. Meade knew that his own army was emotionally and physically exhausted—it had suffered about 23,000 casualties—and most historians believe that he did not want to throw away the Gettysburg victory with an ill-considered second engagement.

On July 14 the Army of Northern Virginia finally crossed the Potomac and resumed their journey back to Virginia. As Lee disappeared over the horizon, Meade reported back to Washington, D.C., that the invader had been vanquished from the North. This message was happily trumpeted by Northern newspapers, which heralded the Battle of Gettysburg as a great triumph and a long-awaited turning point in the war (see "A Northern Newspaper Hails the Victory at Gettysburg," p. 193). Lincoln, though, was beside himself with frustration (see "Lincoln's Unsent Letter to Meade," p. 197). "Great God!" he said upon learning that the Army of Northern Virginia had been permitted to leave the North without another fight. "We had only to stretch forth our hands and they were ours. Our army held the war in the hollow of their hand and would not close it."[13]

## Notes

[1] Longstreet, James. "Lee in Pennsylvania." *The Annals of the War Written by Leading Participants North and South.* Edited by Alexander Kelly McClure. Philadelphia: Times Publishing, 1879, p. 430.

[2] Longstreet, p. 429.

[3] Quoted in Longstreet, p. 429.

[4] Longstreet, p. 429.

[5] Clark, Champ, and the Editors of Time-Life Books. *The Civil War: Gettysburg, The Confederate High Tide.* Alexandria, VA: Time-Life Books, 1985, p. 128.

[6] Miller, William E. "The Cavalry Battle Near Gettysburg." *Battles and Leaders of the Civil War.* Volume 3. Edited by Robert Underwood Johnson and Clarence Clough Buel. New York: Century, 1888, p. 404.

[7] Quoted in Long, A. L., ed. *Memoirs of Robert E. Lee: His Military and Personal History.* New York: Stoddart, 1886, p. 289.

[8] Wert, Jeffrey. "America's Civil War: Robert E. Lee and James Longstreet at Odds at Gettysburg." *HistoryNet.com.* Originally published in *Military History,* August 1994. Retrieved from http://www.history net.com/americas-civil-war-robert-e-lee-and-james-longstreet-at-odds-at-gettysburg.htm.

[9] Quoted in *History of the Nineteenth Regiment Massachusetts Volunteer Infantry, 1861-1865.* Compiled by Ernest Linden Waitt. Salem, MA: Salem Press, 1906, p. 242.

[10] McPherson, James M. *Hallowed Ground: A Walk at Gettysburg.* New York: Crown, 2003, pp. 118-19.

[11] Quoted in Desjardin, Thomas. *These Honored Dead: How the Story of Gettysburg Shaped American Memory.* Cambridge, MA: Da Capo Press, 2003, p. 124.

[12] Quoted in Hess, Earl J. *Pickett's Charge—The Last Attack at Gettysburg.* Chapel Hill: University of North Carolina Press, 2001, p. 236.

[13] Quoted in Nicolay, John George, and John Hay. *Abraham Lincoln: A History.* Vol. 7. New York: The Century Co., 1890, p. 278.

# Chapter Six

# THE WAR
# DRAWS TO A CLOSE

Since [the fall of] Atlanta I have felt as if all were dead within me, forever. We are going to be wiped off the earth.

—Civil War diarist Mary Boykin Chesnut of South Carolina

Gettysburg had changed the entire complexion of the Civil War, or the War of the Rebellion as Southerners preferred to call it. "The myth of Southern military invincibility, built up by early Confederate successes, had endured for more than two years," wrote military historian Edward J. Stackpole. "It was shattered at Gettysburg in three days."[1] Indeed, the Confederate Army never fully recovered from the losses it suffered on that battlefield.

The costly defeat at Gettysburg also weighed heavily on General Robert E. Lee. On August 8, 1863, in fact, he offered his resignation from command of the Army of Northern Virginia in a letter to Confederate president Jefferson Davis. Lee said that such a change made sense, given "the growing failure of my bodily strength" and a possible diminishment of soldierly confidence in his leadership. Davis flatly refused the resignation, though. "To ask me to substitute you by someone … more fit to command, or who would possess more of the confidence of the army or of the reflecting men of the country, is to demand an impossibility,"[2] Davis stated. Lee thus remained in command for the remainder of the war.

## The North Gains Confidence

Davis and Lee, though, now faced a very different war than the one that had existed in the spring of 1863. The same day—July 4—that Lee's Army of

General Ulysses S. Grant at his headquarters in Cold Harbor, Virginia.

Northern Virginia withdrew from Gettysburg, Confederate forces in the Southern city of Vicksburg, Mississippi, capitulated to Union troops after a long siege. The Federal victory at Vicksburg, which had been engineered by General Ulysses S. Grant, commander of the Union's Army of the Tennessee, gave the U.S. Army control over the entire length of the Mississippi River, which was a vital transportation pipeline for troops and military supplies.

The twin blows of Gettysburg and Vicksburg came as an enormous shock to Southerners, who for the first time began to consider the possibility that they would lose the war. "One brief month ago we were apparently at the point of success," lamented Confederate officer Josiah Gorgas in July 1863. "Now the picture is just as sombre as it was bright then.... It seems incredible that human power could effect such a change in so brief a space. Yesterday we rode on the pinnacle of success—today absolute ruin seems to be our portion. The Confederacy totters to its destruction."[3]

Gorgas's fears proved to be well-founded. The Union army gradually took control of ever-greater expanses of Southern territory in late 1863 and 1864, though there were occasional bright spots for the South. Confederate generals, politicians, soldiers, and civilians were heartened by occasional battlefield victories, such as the decisive triumph of General Braxton Bragg's Army of Tennessee over Union general William S. Rosecrans's Army of the Cumberland at Chickamauga, Georgia, on September 19-20, 1863.

Southerners also followed President Lincoln's political problems with avid interest. Lincoln was besieged through much of 1863 by criticisms of his wartime economic and military policies. Some of this opposition was churned up for selfish reasons by Lincoln's political enemies. Other Northerners, however, were genuinely alarmed by some of the administration's actions. They objected to the administration's efforts to silence critical newspapers, for example, as well as its approval of a mandatory military draft for all male citizens between the ages of twenty and forty-five. The latter Conscription Act included a provision that enabled enlistees to avoid serving by hiring a replacement or paying a $300 fee. This loophole gave rise to legitimate complaints that wealthy Northern families were receiving exemptions from the wartime sacrifices that poor and middle-class families were being forced to make.

*"We are not only fighting hostile armies, but a hostile people, and must make old and young, rich and poor, feel the hard hand of war." —Union general William T. Sherman*

Many of these complaints faded in intensity after Gettysburg and Vicksburg, though. These decisive victories renewed the North's faith in its cause, its military generals, and Lincoln himself. This confidence enabled civilian and soldier alike to weather the occasional military setback that followed (such as the Battle of Chickamauga), and it gathered greater strength as Union victories began to pile up in both the Eastern and Western theatres.

Finally, the North's newfound belief in itself and its leaders made Union infantry soldiers, store clerks, and housewives more receptive than ever before to the encouraging words of their president. And few words spoken in wartime were ever as inspiring or meaningful as the ones that Lincoln voiced on November 19, 1863, when he went to Gettysburg for the dedication of the Soldiers' National Cemetery.

## Lincoln's Gettysburg Address

The Soldiers' National Cemetery at Gettysburg had been established as a final resting place for Union troops who had been killed during the three-day battle. The featured speaker at the dedication was Edward Everett, a respected Massachusetts politician and diplomat. Everett spoke for over two hours, and his oration was well-received according to most accounts.

After Everett stepped down, Lincoln stepped forward and delivered remarks that lasted for only two minutes. The president, however, used those two minutes to deliver a speech that is today regarded as a pure and powerful articulation of America's guiding principles of freedom and human equality. Lincoln used the backdrop of the battle site to explain to the gathered crowd how the Civil War was a continuation of the quest to fulfill the ideals and honor the vision of America's Founding Fathers, as expressed in the nation's 1776 Dec-

A dramatic representation of Lincoln's historic address at the dedication of the Gettysburg National Cemetery on November 19, 1863.

laration of Independence. Lincoln also vowed to fight on to make certain that the Union soldiers who fell at Gettysburg "shall not have died in vain" and that "government of the people, by the people, for the people, shall not perish from the earth."

The initial reaction to Lincoln's remarks at Gettysburg depended in large part on the listener. Newspapers across the South and those in the North with ties to the Democratic Party reported that the president gave a boring, tepid speech that fell flat with the audience. Northern newspapers that were more sympathetic to Lincoln and his Republican Party, however, gave much more positive accounts of the speech and its reception. In addition, historians note that at least one person who was present at the ceremony—Edward Everett—recognized the enduring power and majesty of Lincoln's words. "Permit me ... to express my great admiration of the thoughts expressed by you ... at the consecration of the Cemetery," Everett wrote in a letter to the president. "I should be glad, if I could flatter myself that I came as near to the central idea of the occasion, in two hours, as you did in two minutes."[4]

Over time, growing numbers of people grew to share Everett's sentiments about Lincoln's Gettysburg Address. It came to be seen as one of the great speeches in U.S. history, and many of its phrases have assumed an enduring place in American popular culture. Many generations of schoolchildren have studied the address and its meaning, and lawmakers and citizens alike continue to regard it as a document that encapsulates the highest ideals and aspirations of the American people (see "Lincoln's Gettysburg Address," p. 199).

## A Stalemate Turns into a Rout

Lincoln delivered the Gettysburg Address six days before Union forces commanded by Grant claimed victory at the Battle of Chattanooga in Tennessee. In October 1863 Grant had been given authority over all U.S. forces in the war's Western Theatre by Lincoln, and he wasted little time in making use of his expanded arsenal. Using both the Army of the Tennessee (under its new commander, Major General William T. Sherman) and the reconstituted Army of the Cumberland (where Major General George H. Thomas had succeeded Rosecrans), Grant routed Bragg's Army of Tennessee after three days of fighting. This triumph opened the door for Federal armies to march into the heart of the Confederacy.

The winter of 1863-64 brought a lull in the fighting. In the spring, however, the Union army renewed its fierce pressure on the fading Confederate army in both the Eastern and Western theatres. The leading architect of this relentless campaign was Grant, who received command of all Union armies on March 10, 1864. Two months after this promotion, Grant personally led the Army of the Potomac (which was still formally commanded by George Meade) on what came to be known as the Overland Campaign into Confederate territory. Through May and June Grant fought a series of bloody engagements across eastern Virginia against Lee and his Army of Northern Virginia.

Some of these clashes went badly for the invading army, most notably the Battle of Cold Harbor of May 31-June 12. This clash about ten miles northeast of the Confederate capital of Richmond is best known as the battle in which Grant ordered his own version of Pickett's Charge, a disastrous full frontal assault on entrenched Confederate defenses. Years later, Grant wrote in his memoirs that "I have always regretted that the last assault at Cold Harbor was ever made.... No advantage whatever was gained to compensate for the heavy loss we sustained."[5]

The cumulative impact of the Overland Campaign, however, was devastating for Lee, his army, and the South. Grant had more troops, horses, artillery, ammunition, and other supplies than Lee, and he knew it. The Union commander applied relentless pressure on his foe, and the Army of Northern Virginia slowly began to crumble. In mid-June Grant crossed the James River and laid siege to Petersburg, Virginia, a railroad-roadway hub that was the major source of food and other supplies for nearby Richmond. Lee managed to establish defenses around the city, but the siege trapped his army at Petersburg and began to slowly squeeze the life out of it. In the meantime, Union armies further west registered a series of victories that crushed the spirits of Rebel soldiers and civilians alike.

## Sheridan Takes the Shenandoah Valley

The Union commander in the war's Western theatre was General William T. Sherman, and he prosecuted the war with the same skill and ruthlessness that Grant was displaying in Virginia. In August 1864 Sherman's 100,000-man force whipped General John Bell Hood's Army of Tennessee in three different engagements, then laid siege to the strategically vital city of Atlanta. On September 1 Atlanta fell, and with it the confidence of Southerners. Northern cities, meanwhile, celebrated the news of the capture of Atlanta with 100-cannon salutes.[6]

Other events in the summer and fall of 1864 added to the sense that the Confederacy was being pushed to the brink of destruction. On August 5 Union warships under Admiral David Farragut won a sea battle in Alabama's Mobile Bay to close off one of the South's last remaining supply ports. In September and October, the Union's newly organized Army of the Shenandoah, helmed by Major General Philip Sheridan, cleared Lieutenant General Jubal Early and his detachment of Army of Northern Virginia troops out of the fertile Shenandoah Valley. Sheridan then roamed far and wide through the valley, seizing livestock and destroying crops that might otherwise have fed Confederate soldiers.

These triumphs dramatically changed the political environment in the North. During the summer it had appeared that Lincoln might lose his bid for re-election. The exploits of Grant, Sheridan, and Farragut and their men, though, greatly bolstered spirits across the North. On November 8, 1864, Lincoln cruised to re-election, defeating Democratic nominee (and former general of the Army of the Potomac) George B. McClellan.

Major General Philip Sheridan (standing, third from left) poses with some of his officers in the field.

## Sherman's March to the Sea

The winter of 1864-65 brought no relief to the Confederacy or battered Rebel troops. One week after Lincoln's victory, Sherman launched his famous "March to the Sea." Leaving Atlanta's factories, warehouses, and railroad depots in flames, Sherman leisurely moved eastward through Georgia to the coastal city of Savannah. He left a trail of ruin and destruction in his wake. Crops, livestock, and other supplies that Sherman did not confiscate for his own army's consumption were torched or otherwise destroyed. His army also looted private homes, sabotaged railways, and set fire to public buildings and facilities.

105

General William T. Sherman cut a destructive swath through the heart of the Confederacy in late 1864 and early 1865.

This cold-hearted strategy triggered great sorrow and fury among the helpless civilians of Georgia and the wider Confederacy, but Sherman made no apologies. "We are not only fighting hostile armies, but a hostile people, and must make old and young, rich and poor, feel the hard hand of war." Sherman added that "we cannot change the hearts of those people of the South, but we can make war so terrible [and] make them so sick of war that generations would pass away before they would again appeal to it."[7]

Sherman reached Savannah in mid-December, and he took control of the city on December 21. Sherman then sent a telegraph to Washington, D.C., in which he described the captured city as a Christmas present for Lincoln.

## Lee Surrenders and the Confederacy Falls

The news was just as grim for the rebellion in other parts of the South. On December 16 a coalition of Union forces (including two brigades of African-American infantry) led by Major General George H. Thomas routed Hood's Army of Tennessee at the Battle of Nashville. "The victory had been complete," wrote historian Bruce Catton. "Hood's army was shattered beyond repair."[8]

In the first months of 1865 the Federal armies finished the job. They roamed across the length and breadth of the sagging Confederacy with little opposition, seizing control of such targets as Charleston, South Carolina (where the first shots of the war had been fired), the South Carolina capital of Columbia, and the port city of Wilmington, North Carolina. At the beginning of April Lee evacuated the hungry remnants of his Army of Northern Virginia from Petersburg and Richmond after enduring nine months of siege. On April 2 the Confederate government fled Richmond, and people of the city responded to their departure with an ugly spasm of looting and arson. One day later Grant and his men marched into the smoking capital. "Our army is demoralized and the people panic stricken," wrote one South Carolinian. "To fight longer seems to be madness."[9]

The ruins of the Richmond & Petersburg Railroad Depot after civilian rioting.

Lee came to the same conclusion a week later. Lee and his army—now reduced to fewer than 30,000 men—had fled west out of Petersburg and Richmond. He hoped to reunite in North Carolina with the battered Army of Tennessee, the last Confederate force of any size left in the field. But Lee's desperate flight came to an end in less than a week. After traveling about ninety miles the Army of Northern Virginia found itself trapped on all sides by Union soldiers from

107

Artist's rendering of the setting at Appomattox Court House, where Lee (seated at center left) surrendered to Grant (seated at center right).

Grant and Sheridan's armies. "Lee couldn't go forward," said a member of his infantry. "He couldn't go backward, and he couldn't go sideways."[10]

On April 7 Lee ordered his men to halt at Appomattox Court House, a village in central Virginia. Two days later, Lee and Grant and their respective staffs met at a small farmhouse in Appomattox and negotiated the terms of the surrender of the Army of Northern Virginia. By all accounts, the meeting between the two great generals was warm, respectful, and cordial, in part because Grant offered generous terms.

Lee's signing of these surrender papers is widely regarded as the event that brought the Civil War to a close, although the last Confederate regiments did not lay down their weapons until June 2. Grant recalled that when Lee left the farmhouse to inform his loyal men about the terms of their surrender, "I felt like anything rather than rejoicing at the downfall of a foe who had fought so long and valiantly, and had suffered so much for a cause, though that cause was, I believe, one of the worst for which a people ever fought."[11]

## Notes

[1] Stackpole, Edward J. *They Met at Gettysburg.* Harrisburg, PA: Stackpole Books, 1956, p. 44.
[2] Quoted in Lee, Fitzhugh. *General Lee.* New York: Appleton, 1894, p. 311.

[3] Vandiver, Frank E., ed. *The Civil War Diary of General Josiah Gorgas.* Mobile: University of Alabama Press, 1947, p. 55.

[4] "A Gracious Compliment." Letter from Edward Everett to President Lincoln, November 20, 1863. *My LOC (Library of Congress): Gettysburg Address.* Retrieved from http://myloc.gov/Exhibitions/gettysburg address/exhibitionitems/Pages/Transcription.aspx?ex=1@d6db09e6-d424-4113-8bd2-c89bd42b1fad@ 9&asset=d6db09e6-d424-4113-8bd2-c89bd42b1fad:4ab8a6e6-eb9e-40f8-9144-6a417c034a17:115.

[5] Grant, Ulysses S. *Personal Memoirs of Ulysses S. Grant,* Vol. 2. New York: Charles L. Webster, 1886, pp. 276-77.

[6] McPherson, James M. *Battle Cry of Freedom: The Civil War Era.* New York: Oxford University Press, 1988, pp. 774-75.

[7] Quoted in McPherson, p. 809.

[8] Catton, Bruce. *This Hallowed Ground: A History of the Civil War.* 1955. Reprint. New York: Vintage, 2012, p. 368.

[9] Quoted in Barrett, John G. *Sherman's March Through the Carolinas.* Chapel Hill: University of North Carolina Press, 1956, p. 96.

[10] Quoted in Ward, Geoffrey, with Ric Burns and Ken Burns. *The Civil War.* New York: Vintage Books, 1994, p. 305.

[11] Grant, p. 489.

mony, and in no way to oppose the policy of the State or General Government directed to that object."[1]

## A New Nation Takes Shape

Sectional tensions remained high throughout the so-called Reconstruction era, which ran from the close of the war to 1877. During this time, a wide range of Reconstruction programs were implemented by the federal government to repair the war's economic and social damage in the South and slowly bring the ex-Confederate states back into the Union fold. Reconstruction also included many provisions designed to protect the lives and rights of newly free African Americans.

Reconstruction collapsed after twelve years, though, under the weight of white Southern hostility and Northern weariness with all the postwar bickering. Once the federal government curtailed its involvement in the affairs of the former Confederate states, white lawmakers all across the South passed "Jim Crow" laws that stripped generations of blacks of basic rights and kept them uneducated, impoverished, and powerless. Stories of lynchings and other barbaric treatment of African Americans proliferated across the South, providing brutal evidence that the racism that had sanctioned and rationalized slavery continued to afflict the region.

*"[The Civil War] was fought in our own backyard. Or front yard if you will, and you're not apt to forget something that happened on your own property." — Southern Civil War historian Shelby Foote.*

Other far-reaching consequences of the war also became clear with the passage of time. Political power in the United States, for example, shifted decisively to the North. Prior to the war, a sizable majority of U.S. presidents, speakers of the House of Representatives, presidents pro tem of the Senate, and Supreme Court justices had hailed from the slaveholding South. For half a century after the war, though, all of the House speakers and Senate presidents pro tem came from the North, as did more than 80 percent of Supreme Court appointees. Meanwhile, it took more than a century before a resident of an ex-Confederate state (Jimmy Carter of Georgia) was elected president.

The Civil War also firmly established the authority of the federal government over state legislatures. The postwar era saw national agencies assume control over a wide range of policy areas that had once been the sole or primary province of states. Federal income taxes were gradually introduced and strengthened, as were systems for national banking, national defense, and centralized management and conservation of national forests and other natural resources judged to be the common property of the American people. "Eleven of the first twelve amendments of the Constitution had limited the powers of the national government," observed historian James M. McPherson. "Six of the next seven, beginning with the Thirteenth Amendment [outlawing slavery] in 1865, vastly expanded those powers at the expense of the states."[2]

Yet despite all of the lingering bitterness and the fresh flare-ups of racial hatred and sectional distrust, the United States was slowly—at times agonizingly—stitched back together. "The wonder is not that the job was done so imperfectly, but that it was done at all," wrote historian Bruce Catton. "For it was done, finally; if not finished, at least set on the road to completion."[3] And as the Union was cobbled back together out of the wreckage of the war, the United States strode forth into the twentieth century as one of the world's great economic and military powers.

Gettysburg thus came to be seen as an event that shaped the course of millions of lives in America and around the world for generations to come. If Lee had been victorious at Gettysburg and the Confederate states had succeeded in their quest for independence, how would major historical events like World War I and World War II have unfolded? Could German dictator Adolf Hitler have been defeated in 1945 if the industrial and military might of a reunited America not been brought to bear against him? And how would the Union and Confederacy have evolved in a world in which their peoples did not live and work together under the banner of the American flag? "What if the coal in Kentucky and West Virginia had been separated by national boundaries and tariffs from Pennsylvania steel and factories in the East?" asked historian Thomas A. Desjardin. "How quickly would technology have advanced without the combined drive and intellect of a whole United States? No atom bomb, no space program, slower moves toward automobiles, airplanes, computers?"[4] The answers to these questions are, of course, unknowable.

## Healing and Reconciliation

World events during the first half of the twentieth century served to soothe (but not eliminate) some of the lingering Southern feelings of anger and bitterness over the war. Most Southerners were grateful for the federal New Deal policies of President (and New York native) Franklin D. Roosevelt, which helped them survive the Great Depression of the 1930s. In addition, the feelings of patri-

## Preserving Civil War Battlefields

**B**y the late nineteenth century, the enduring public fascination with the Civil War had convinced the U.S. Congress to commemorate four major battlefields as national military parks. These four parks—Chickamauga and Chattanooga (established in 1890), Shiloh (1894), Gettysburg (1895), and Vicksburg (1899)—became the foundation for an extensive network of preserved Civil War sites across the eastern United States. The importance of these parks was underscored in 1896, when the U.S. Supreme Court issued a unanimous decision (*United States v. Gettysburg Electric Ry. Co.*) affirming the federal government's right to 1) remove a private trolley line that had been built over part of the Gettysburg battlefield and 2) take ownership of the entire battlefield to protect it from development. "The battle of Gettysburg was one of the great battles of the world," stated the decision.

> The importance of the issue involved in the contest of which this great battle was a part cannot be overestimated. The existence of the government itself, and the perpetuity of our institutions depended upon the result…. Can it be that the government is without power to preserve the land, and properly mark out the various sites upon which this struggle took place? Can it not … take possession of the field of battle, in the name and for the benefit of all the citizens of the country? … Such a use seems necessarily not only a public use, but one so closely connected with the welfare of the republic itself as to be within the powers granted Congress by the Constitution for the purpose of protecting and preserving the whole country.

Today, the National Park Service system includes sixteen Civil War battlefields that have been designated as national historic landmarks and fifty-eight Civil War-related military parks and historic sites. These sites have been carefully preserved and their histories painstakingly documented so as to inform visitors about their importance in American history. The Chickamauga and Chattanooga National Military Park, for example, features 1,400 monuments and markers within its boundaries, while the grounds of Gettysburg National Military Park are dotted with 1,300 memorials, monuments, and markers. Private organizations such as the Civil War Trust have also worked tirelessly to acquire historically significant lands and protect them from development.

### Sources

"The Civil War: 150 Years. A National Park Service Sesquicentennial Commemoration." *National Park Service* [online], February 2, 2011. Retrieved from http://www .nps.gov/features/waso/cw150th/index.html.

Lee, Ronald F. "The Origin and Evolution of the National Military Park Idea." *National Park Service* [online], 1973. Retrieved from http://www.nps.gov/history/history/online _books/history_military/index.htm.

The Wheatfield Monument at Gettysburg National Military Park.

Gettysburg veterans from the Confederate (left) and Union armies shake hands at the 1913 reunion.

otism and unity stoked by America's entrance into World War I (in 1917) and World War II (in 1941) helped Southerners once again see Northerners not just as Yankees, but as fellow Americans. In 1945, in fact, the people of Vicksburg, Mississippi, ended a ban on Fourth of July celebrations that had been in effect since 1863, when Ulysses S. Grant and his Yankee army seized control of the city.

Another powerful symbol of sectional reconciliation came in 1913, when 53,000 elderly veterans of Gettysburg returned to the battlefield for a week-long reunion. The ceremonies and celebrations at the event emphasized the bravery and heroism of the soldiers, and took pains to avoid discussions of the ideological and philosophical differences that had caused the war in the first place. The event was by all accounts a big success, and it closed with a special July 4 address delivered by President Woodrow Wilson (see "Woodrow Wilson Addresses Civil War Veterans at Gettysburg," p. 200).

The number of living Gettysburg veterans fell sharply in subsequent years, as illness and old age took their inevitable toll. Nonetheless, in 1938 a seventy-fifth anniversary commemoration of the Battle of Gettysburg was held at Gettysburg National Military Park. This event featured an address by President Roosevelt to an audience of 250,000 that included more than 1,800 Civil War veterans and two dozen or so actual survivors of Gettysburg, all of whom were well over ninety years of age. "Lincoln spoke in solace for all who fought upon this field," said Roosevelt, "and the years have laid their balm upon their wounds. Men who wore the blue and men who wore the gray are here together, a fragment spared by time. They are brought here by the memories of old divided loyalties, but they meet here in united loyalty to a united cause which the unfolding years have made it easier to see. All of them we honor, not asking under which flag they fought then—thankful that they stand together under one flag now."[5]

## Making Sense of the War

Amid the healing and reconciliation, the Civil War and its most titanic battles—Gettysburg above all—came to occupy an ever more prominent place in the minds of the nation's citizenry. "The Civil War left America with a legend and a haunting memory," wrote Catton.

> These had to do less with things that remained than with the things that had been lost.... North and South together shared in this, for if the consciousness of defeat afflicted only one of the two sections, both knew that something greatly cherished was gone forever, whether that something was only a remembered smile on the face of a boy who had died or was the great shadow of a way of life that had been destroyed.... Knowing the cruelty and insane destructiveness of war as well as any people who ever lived, they nevertheless kept looking backward, and they put a strange gloss of romance on what they saw, cherishing the haunted overtones it had left.[6]

Indeed, Americans proved unable—or unwilling—to forget the war. Publishers released hundreds of Civil War memoirs and historical works in the 1880s and 1890s. Many of these works provided powerful and poignant insights into the wartime experiences of famous generals and ordinary foot soldiers alike. Others, such as the memoirs of Gettysburg participants like Union general Dan Sickles and Confederate general Jubal Early, were written with an eye toward burnishing the authors' places in the history books—and muddy-ing the reputations of fellow officers whom they disliked. Early, for example, worked relentlessly to paint General James Longstreet, with whom he had a long-running feud, as the man most responsible for Lee's defeat at Gettysburg.

Early was also a prominent disciple of what came to be known as the "Lost Cause" movement in the South. Lost Cause advocates painted an idyllic picture of the prewar South, with slavery pushed deep into the background. They also depicted Confederate generals and soldiers as noble, brave, and chivalrous figures who were only narrowly defeated by treachery and the overwhelming size and scale of the Northern war machine. This version of history was widely embraced across the South, and it remains popular among many Southerners today.

Not surprisingly, the pivotal Battle of Gettysburg—and Pickett's final doomed assault on the North's defenses there—became special subjects of interest to Lost Causers. "Pickett's Charge provided [an] important element of the Lost Cause mythology in that it served to reduce the entire Civil War to one critical and momentous instant while also depicting a superior quality among Southern soldiers," wrote historian Thomas A. Desjardin.

> It provided a critical moment in time when some fatal human flaw, rather than the determining will of God, could and did seal the Confederacy's fate. The more they elevated the importance of the battle and particularly the charge, the easier it was to accept this idea. Further, the more desperate and suicidal the image of the charge became, the greater was the idea that Southern soldiers exhibited bravery, heroism, and commitment to their cause, qual-ities that they presumably held in ways far superior to the Yankees.[7]

Many Southerners say that their particular fascination with the Civil War and its complex themes of valor and heartbreak will always remain strong. "It was fought in our own backyard," explained Southern Civil War historian Shel-by Foote. "Or front yard if you will, and you're not apt to forget something that happened on your own property."[8]

## A Milestone in American Memory and Culture

In the end, though, events like the Battle of Gettysburg were too big to be defined only by Southerners flying the Lost Cause banner. Gettysburg captured the imagination of millions of other Americans as well. "To many southerners, it is the place where a dream met its death," acknowledged Desjardin. But he added that "to many Americans, Gettysburg is the place where our nation was saved."[9]

Gettysburg is also a battle that enhanced the reputations of both sides. Southerners held different perspectives on the reasons for Lee's defeat—but they *all* took solace in the fact that the Yankees who occupied the heights above Gettysburg fought valiantly throughout the three-day battle. Northerners, meanwhile, may have condemned the "treasonous" attitudes of the Rebels—but they also marveled at the bravery and dedication of the Confederate troops who crashed again and again against the Union's fearsome armaments at Devil's Den and Culp's Hill and Cemetery Ridge. "The battlefield memorial at Gettysburg and the popular memory of the battle eventually glorified all the dead because they had exemplified what many people believed were distinctly American traits such as self-sacrifice, courage, and a willingness to fight for one's convictions," wrote historian Amy J. Kinsel. "Americans who could recite Lincoln's Gettysburg Address also stood in awe of Pickett's Charge."[10]

After the war ended, former Confederate general Jubal Early became a leading proponent of the "Lost Cause" movement.

Many of the men who fought at Gettysburg (and in other major Civil War engagements) thus became larger-than-life figures, and so they remain. A century and a half after the Army of Northern Virginia and the Army of the Potomac met at Gettysburg, the names of revered men like Lee, Pickett, Longstreet, Chamberlain, and Reynolds continue to exist in a world that shifts back and forth between historical fact and inspiring mythology. The mythology swirling around the Civil War became so great, in fact, that English historian Denis William Brogan commented that "the United States is the only country since the Middle Ages that has created a legend to set beside the story of Achilles, Robin Hood, Roland, and [King] Arthur."[11]

Gettysburg also contributed to the legend of Lincoln, who is regarded today by both historians and the American public as the greatest of U.S. presidents. Over the years, in fact, his Gettysburg Address came to be seen as such

The southern wall of the Lincoln Memorial in Washington, D.C., is inscribed with the words of the Gettysburg Address.

## Joshua Lawrence Chamberlain (1828-1914)
*Union Officer Who Led the Defense of Little Round Top at Gettysburg*

Joshua Lawrence Chamberlain was born in Brewer, Maine, on September 8, 1828. He was the eldest of five children born to Joshua and Sarah Brastow Chamberlain. His father was a military veteran who hoped that his oldest son would follow in his footsteps, while his mother encouraged him to consider a career as a minister. In the end, however, Chamberlain pursued a third course. In 1848 he enrolled at Bowdoin College in Brunswick, Maine, where he studied under Calvin Stowe, husband of the famed abolitionist author Harriet Beecher Stowe. After earning his bachelor's degree in 1852, he decided to continue his education at Bangor Theological Seminary in Bangor, Maine.

The mid-1850s were years of transition for Chamberlain. In 1855 he married Fannie Adams, with whom he eventually had five children (three of whom died in infancy). That same year, Chamberlain left Bangor to accept a teaching position at Bowdoin. Fluent in several languages, Chamberlain served primarily as a professor of languages and rhetoric. He was by all accounts popular with students and fellow faculty alike.

### Heeding the Call to War

When the Civil War broke out in April 1861, Chamberlain became a vocal supporter of the Union—and an ardent believer that privileged, educated Northerners such as himself needed to join their working-class countrymen in serving their country in the army. His views caused some discomfort on the Bowdoin campus, and he was quickly granted a two-year leave of absence. Chamberlain subsequently volunteered for military service, and on August 8, 1862, he officially became a lieutenant colonel in the newly raised 20th Maine regiment. Around this same time, Chamberlain's younger brother Thomas also was appointed an officer with the 20th Maine, which was part of the V Corps of the Army of the Potomac, the Union's main army in the conflict's Eastern theatre.

Upon joining the army Chamberlain became an avid reader of various military works. The scholar-turned-soldier also benefited greatly from the mentorship of his regimental commander, Colonel Adelbert Ames. Chamberlain and the 20th Maine were largely held out of combat at the fearsome Battle of Antietam on September 17, 1862, in Sharpsburg, Maryland, but they were in the thick of the action at the Battle of Fredericksburg that December. Years later, Chamberlain wrote in his memoirs about spending a freezing night on the Fredericksburg battlefield hunkered down behind a wall of corpses that offered protection from enemy fire. The following May, a smallpox outbreak in the regiment prevented the 20th Maine from being deployed at the Battle of Chancellorsville. One month later, Chamberlain was promoted to colonel of the regiment, replacing Ames, who had been made a brigade commander.

## Valor at Little Round Top

Chamberlain and the 20th Maine achieved lasting fame at the Battle of Gettysburg, which raged outside the small town of Gettysburg, Pennsylvania, from July 1-3, 1863. On the second day of the battle, Confederate troops of General Robert E. Lee's Army of Northern Virginia assailed Union defensive lines with tremendous force. As the bloodshed escalated, a Union officer discovered that a hill at the southernmost end of the Union position had been left completely undefended. If the Rebels occupied that hill—known as Little Round Top—they would be able to strafe the Union's already struggling defenses with devastating artillery fire.

Four Union regiments were frantically sent to take up positions on the western slopes of Little Round Top. Chamberlain and the 20th Maine were assigned to the far left flank (southern end) of the hill, thus establishing the unit as the southernmost regiment of the Army of the Potomac's entire defensive formation. Mere minutes after Chamberlain and his men had taken up their positions, Confederate infantry came pouring up the hillsides. Hours of intense combat ensued, for the Rebels knew that if they could cave in the enemy's left flank, the Union's entire defenses would be in jeopardy. But the 20th Maine never crumbled. Chamberlain and his men warded off every assault, and when they ran short of ammunition, Chamberlain ordered a bayonet attack that cleared Little Round Top of enemy forces.

This heroic defense of Little Round Top gradually became one of the most famous clashes at the Battle of Gettysburg. More than a century later, in fact, it was prominently featured in several popular media treatments of the Battle of Gettysburg, including Michael Shaara's novel *The Killer Angels* (1974), the Ken

Burns documentary *The Civil War* (1990), and the feature film *Gettysburg* (1993). Chamberlain, who received two slight wounds at Little Round Top, eventually received the Congressional Medal of Honor for his performance at Gettysburg.

## Witness to Lee's Surrender

After Gettysburg Chamberlain struggled with bouts of malaria and dysentery. He was taken off active duty in November 1863 and spent several months regaining his strength at home in Maine. Chamberlain resumed command of the 20th Maine in May 1864, just in time to lead the unit in the bloody Battle of Cold Harbor.

In June 1864 Chamberlain was promoted to brigade command. Less than two weeks later he was seriously wounded in the Army of the Potomac's initial assault on Petersburg, Virginia. Shot in the right hip and groin, Chamberlain was carried from the front lines to a battlefield surgeon who declared that the wound was mortal. Newspapers in Maine even published obituaries, and General Ulysses S. Grant approved what he believed to be a posthumous promotion of Chamberlain to the rank of brigadier general. Chamberlain did not succumb to his injuries, however. Showing grit and resilience, he slowly recovered, and in November 1864 he returned to active service (to the dismay of his wife, who desperately wanted him to return home).

In early 1865 Chamberlain became commander of the First Brigade of the 1st division of V Corps. It was in this capacity that he participated in the Appomattox Campaign—Grant's successful effort to squeeze the last embers of resistance out of Lee's tattered Army of Northern Virginia. On April 9 Lee finally surrendered to Grant at Appomattox Court House, Virginia. Three days later, Chamberlain was given the honor of commanding the troops that formally accepted the surrender of the Army of Northern Virginia's infantry.

## Governor of Maine and President of Bowdoin

Chamberlain's enthusiasm for public service and his illustrious military record—he participated in more than twenty battles and skirmishes, was wounded six times, and retired as a major general—made him an extremely attractive political candidate. In 1866 he ran for governor of Maine as a Republican and was elected by an overwhelming margin. He served four one-year terms as governor before accepting the presidency of Bowdoin College. Chamberlain led the school from 1871 to 1883, when health problems associated with his war injuries forced him to step down.

In the 1880s and 1890s Chamberlain occupied himself with various business ventures, even though his war injuries left him in a state of near-constant pain and discomfort. He also wrote extensively about his wartime experiences and was an active member of Civil War veterans' organizations. Chamberlain died on February 24, 1914, in Portland, Maine, finally succumbing to complications from the war wounds he had incurred a half-century earlier.

## Sources

Chamberlain, Joshua Lawrence. *Bayonet! Forward: My Civil War Reminiscences.* Gettysburg, PA: Stan Clark Military Books, 1994.

Longacre, Edward G. *Joshua Chamberlain: The Soldier and the Man.* Boston, MA: Da Capo Press, 2003.

Trulock, Alice Rains. *In the Hands of Providence: Joshua L. Chamberlain and the American Civil War.* Chapel Hill: University of North Carolina Press, 1992.

Wallace, Willard M. *Soul of the Lion: A Biography of General Joshua L. Chamberlain.* 1960. Reprint. Gettysburg, PA: Stan Clark Military Books, 1991.

## Ulysses S. Grant (1822-1885)
*General-in-Chief of Union Forces During the Last Year of the War*

Hiram Ulysses Grant was born on April 27, 1822, in Point Pleasant, Ohio, a small village along the banks of the Ohio River. His parents were Jesse Root Grant, who worked as a tanner, and Hannah Simpson Grant. As a youth, Grant was quiet and not particularly dedicated to his studies. Nonetheless, in 1839 his father managed to use social connections to get him enrolled at West Point Military Academy, the country's main army officer training school. It was during this nomination process that Grant mistakenly received the middle initial "S," which was the first letter in his mother's maiden name. Rather than kick up a fuss over the error in the paperwork, Grant shrugged and accepted the middle initial for the rest of his life.

Grant attended West Point reluctantly. He was not at all sure that he wanted to pursue a military career. But while he did not distinguish himself academically at West Point, he also did not perform so poorly as to flunk out. In fact, Grant developed a reputation as perhaps the finest horseman of his entire class.

### A Nomadic Life in the Army

When Grant graduated from West Point in 1843, he initially intended to serve out his obligatory military service and then return to civilian life. With the passage of time, however, Grant became more accepting of a prospective career in the U.S. Army. His first posting was with the 4th Infantry, where he served as regimental quartermaster at the rank of brevet second lieutenant. After brief stints in Missouri and Louisiana, in 1845 Grant went with the 4th Infantry to Texas, where they were part of the U.S. Army's occupation force in the territory. The dispute with Mexico over ownership of Texas exploded into war the following year.

Grant served with distinction in the Mexican-American War, which lasted from 1846 to 1848, when Mexico was forced to relinquish its claims to Texas and much of the modern American West. Grant's bravery in several battles was all the more noteworthy given that he personally thought that the war against Mexico was an unjust one. On August 22, 1848, he married Julia Boggs Dent, the daughter of a wealthy Missouri plantation owner. They eventually had four children together.

Grant and his wife spent the next six years leading a nomadic existence, moving from assignments that took him all the way from Detroit and New York State to the Oregon Territory. In 1853 he was promoted to the rank of captain, but one year later he abruptly resigned his commission and returned to civilian life. The exact circumstances behind Grant's resignation remain murky. Some historians assert that the resignation may have been forced by superiors unhappy with Grant's alcohol consumption. Others point out that Grant had left his family behind when he went to Oregon in 1852, and that he had been unable to raise enough funds for them to join him out west. Grant's desire to be reunited with his family, then, may have also been a decisive factor in his decision. From this point forward, however, Grant was dogged by gossip that he had a drinking problem.

The next several years were difficult ones for Grant and his family. After leaving the army Grant worked variously as a tanner, farmer, real estate agent, and bill collector. None of these pursuits worked out very well, though, and financial worries dogged the family throughout the latter half of the 1850s. The Grants also owned several slaves during this time; Julia inherited ownership of four slaves, and Grant himself received a slave from his father-in-law. In 1859, though, Grant granted freedom to the slave he personally owned.

## Taking Up Arms for the Union Cause

When the Civil War broke out in the spring of 1861, Grant was working in his father's leather store in Galena, Illinois. He immediately offered his services to the U.S. Army, but his expectations of receiving a regular field command went unfulfilled. Instead, he accepted a request from the governor of Illinois to train and command a regiment of volunteers.

By the close of 1861 Grant had been promoted to the position of brigadier general in the Army of the Missouri, in the war's Western Theatre. In early 1862 Grant played an important role in the capture of two strategically vital Confederate forts on the Cumberland and Tennessee rivers. These victories enabled Union forces to penetrate deep into Confederate territory and caught the attention of President Abraham Lincoln. Lincoln's War Department subsequently promoted Grant to the rank of major general and gave him command of a nearly 50,000-man force that became known as the Army of the Tennessee.

Grant's tenure as major general got off to a rough start when Confederate forces surprised him at the Battle of Shiloh in April 1862. Grant recovered and managed to fight the enemy to a bloody draw at Shiloh, but accounts of the clash still prompted some calls for his demotion. Lincoln bluntly turned aside these demands, declaring that "I can't spare this man—he fights."

Grant proved that the president was wise to stick by him. In July 1863 he captured Vicksburg, Mississippi, after a long siege. This victory, combined with the Federal occupation of New Orleans the previous year, gave the Union control of the entire length of the Mississippi River. It also gave Grant and other Union commanders in the war's Western Theatre a pathway deep into the Confederacy. In November 1863 Grant's army seized control of another major Southern city—Chattanooga, Tennessee.

## General of All Union Forces

Grant's exploits out west convinced Lincoln to name him general-in-chief of the entire Union army in March 1864. Grant immediately directed General William T. Sherman to carry out an invasion of the South designed to shatter the morale of the enemy. Meanwhile, Grant headed east to join the Army of the Potomac, the Union's single largest army.

Once Grant arrived in Virginia, he left General George G. Meade in command of the Army of the Potomac's day-to-day affairs. Grant made it clear, though, that the army's movements and battle strategies would be under his overall direction. Over the course of the next year, Grant relentlessly pursued Confederate general Robert E. Lee and his Army of Northern Virginia, the biggest and best of the Confederate armies in the field.

Grant suffered occasional setbacks in his quest to run down Lee, but he used his superior manpower and military resources to slowly establish a chokehold on the Army of Northern Virginia. By the end of 1864 Lee's troops were bottled up in Petersburg and Richmond, Virginia. Meanwhile, Sherman had burned a destructive path through the middle of the Confederacy and Union forces under the command of Philip Sheridan had seized control of western Virginia's strategically vital Shenandoah Valley. As the calendar flipped to the year

1865, it was clear to most people in both the North and South that the Confederacy was tottering toward collapse.

On April 9, 1865, Lee personally surrendered to Grant at Appomattox Court House, Virginia. Grant offered generous terms for Lee and his men to lay down their arms, and Lee gratefully accepted. Grant's defeat of the Army of Northern Virginia marked the final death knell for the Confederacy, though isolated bands of Rebel troops refused to acknowledge defeat for several more weeks.

## Eighteenth President of the United States

After the war concluded, Grant's status as the North's greatest military hero of the conflict was unquestioned. He was tapped to oversee military affairs in the South during Reconstruction, and he also served as secretary of war from August 12, 1867, to January 14, 1868. In 1868 he received the presidential nomination of the Republican Party, which was eager to capitalize on his popularity. He easily won the election that November, defeating Democratic nominee Horatio Seymour. When Grant was inaugurated on March 4, 1869, and become the country's eighteenth president, he also became the youngest American ever to occupy the Oval Office to that point.

Grant's presidency was a troubled one, although he did manage to gain re-election in November 1872. He was a man of honesty and integrity, but many of his political appointments did not share these qualities, and his administration was riddled with scandals. Grant also struggled to come up with an effective and consistent set of Reconstruction policies, though he did sign the Fifteenth Amendment into law in 1870, extending voting rights to all Americans regardless of race. Finally, Grant presided over an 1873 economic panic triggered by Wall Street financiers who ran wild during his two terms in office. For much of his time in the White House, charge critics, Grant seemed bewildered about how to handle the challenges confronting the nation and passive about implementing financial and political reforms that might have improved the picture.

Collectively, these problems and issues drained public support for Grant's presidency, although his wartime service remained widely appreciated across the North. In 1876 the Republicans decided to nominate Rutherford B. Hayes for the presidency, denying Grant an opportunity to run for a third term. Hayes went on to win the presidency over Democratic nominee Samuel Tilden in one of the most controversial presidential elections in U.S. history.

After leaving the Oval Office, Grant spent several years traveling the world with his wife. This tour was organized around visits to various heads of state, who welcomed the couple with great pomp and ceremony. Upon returning to the United States he became a partner in a New York City financial firm. Grant hoped that this new business venture would finally give him the financial security that had eluded him all his life, but in 1884 the firm went bankrupt due to embezzlement by his partner. Grant was forced to sell nearly all of his mementoes from the Civil War in order to pay off his debts.

Around this same time Grant was diagnosed with throat cancer. Knowing that his time was short, he approached his friend Mark Twain, who helped him secure a hefty contract from a publisher for his memoirs. Grant spent the last months of his life recounting his early life, Civil War experiences, and years in the White House. Grant died in Mount MacGregor, New York, on July 23, 1885, a few days after finishing the project. His memoirs were published a few weeks later. The two-volume set continues to be regarded today as among the best of the nation's presidential memoirs. It also was a big commercial success that provided Grant's wife and family the financial security that he had long sought to provide for them.

## Sources

Brands, H. W. *The Man Who Saved the Union: Ulysses S. Grant in War and Peace.* New York: Doubleday, 2012.

Grant, Ulysses S. *Personal Memoirs of U. S. Grant.* 2 vols. New York: Charles L. Webster & Company, 1885.

McPherson, James M. *Battle Cry of Freedom: The Civil War Era.* New York: Oxford University Press, 1988.

Waugh, Joan. *U. S. Grant: American Hero, American Myth.* Chapel Hill: University of North Carolina Press, 2009.

## Winfield Scott Hancock (1824-1886)
*Union General at the Battle of Gettysburg*

Winfield Scott Hancock and his twin brother, Hilary, were born in Montgomery Square, Pennsylvania, on February 14, 1824. His parents, Benjamin Franklin Hancock and Elizabeth Hoxworth Hancock, named Winfield Scott after a famous American general in the War of 1812. Young Winfield's father supported his family as a schoolteacher and lawyer.

In 1840 Hancock enrolled at the U.S. Military Academy at West Point, New York. After graduating in 1844 he was posted (with the rank of second lieutenant) to Indian Territory in the southern Great Plains. Hancock then took part in the Mexican-American War of 1846-48 as an infantry officer.

After the Mexican-American War concluded, Hancock served as a quartermaster (supply officer) at several military posts across the country. In 1850 he married Almira "Allie" Russell, with whom he had two children. By the close of the decade Hancock had received a promotion to captain and been transferred to a military post in Los Angeles, California. During his time in Los Angeles Hancock became best friends with fellow officer Lewis Armistead, whom he would face at Gettysburg.

### A Swift Rise Through the Ranks

When the Civil War broke out in early 1861, Hancock bid farewell to Armistead and his other military friends from the South, nearly all of whom resigned their U.S. Army commissions in order to join the newly forming Confederate Army. Hancock was a firm Democrat, and so he was not a supporter of the new president, Republican Abraham Lincoln. But he also believed strongly in the importance of preserving the Union, so Hancock never wavered in his dedication to the U.S. Army.

Hancock soon received orders to report to Washington, D.C. When he arrived in the capital in September 1861 he was given command of an infantry brigade in the Army of the Potomac, the Union's largest military force in the

East. Hancock quickly established himself as one of the Union's smartest and steadiest brigadier generals. His talents became more widely recognized after the May 1862 Battle of Williamsburg, in which his brigade performed with great skill and valor.

From this point forward Hancock was in the thick of some of the war's heaviest fighting. In the bloody Battle of Antietam in September 1862 he assumed field command of the Army of the Potomac's 1st Division, II Corps when Major General Israel B. Richardson was mortally wounded. Hancock kept the position after the fighting ended, and in November he was formally promoted to major general of the Union's volunteer corps. Hancock also saw heavy action at the December 1862 Battle of Fredericksburg (in which he was wounded) and the May 1863 Battle of Chancellorsville (where he was again wounded).

The Battle of Chancellorsville was an unmitigated disaster for General Joseph Hooker and the Army of the Potomac, which suffered a humiliating defeat at the hands of Confederate general Robert E. Lee and his Army of Northern Virginia. But the rout would have been even more devastating had Hancock and his division not provided excellent cover for Hooker's retreat. On May 22, 1863, Hancock was promoted to commander of the Second Corps of the Army of the Potomac.

## An Unyielding Stand at Gettysburg

In early July 1863 the Army of Northern Virginia and the Army of the Potomac ripped into one another once again, this time outside the quiet town of Gettysburg, Pennsylvania. The Battle of Gettysburg began in earnest on July 1 and raged on for three days, during which time Hancock repeatedly proved his mettle. When the advance elements of both armies first became engaged at Gettysburg, newly installed Army of the Potomac commander George G. Meade sent Hancock to the front to gauge whether Gettysburg would be a good place to make a military stand. Meade also gave Hancock the authority to supervise all Federal troop movements on the battlefield, even though he was not the senior officer in the field. Hancock confirmed that Meade's forces were in good position to face Lee, and he spent the evening of July 1 solidifying the Union's defensive lines.

On July 2 the four corps under Hancock's field command played pivotal roles in warding off Confederate assaults up and down the Union lines. One day later, Hancock's men helped repulse "Pickett's Charge," a final attempt by Lee to claim victory. It was during this offensive that Armistead, Hancock's best

135

friend, was mortally wounded. The failure of Pickett's Charge turned the Battle of Gettysburg into a Federal victory that helped change the war's momentum in favor of the Union.

Hancock was unable to fully enjoy the victory at Gettysburg, however. He had been severely wounded in the thigh during the final day's action. It took him several months to recover from the injury. Hancock spent part of his convalescence assisting with Federal military recruiting efforts, but he was greatly relieved when he was cleared to resume his command of the Second Corps of the Army of the Potomac in the spring of 1864.

## Return to Action

By the time Hancock returned to action, Union general-in-chief Ulysses S. Grant was traveling with the Army of the Potomac. Meade remained nominally in charge of the army, but the force was clearly under Grant's control. Hancock performed well in Grant's May-June 1864 Overland Campaign into Virginia, but he suffered heavy casualties to his corps during Grant's disastrous offensive at Cold Harbor.

During this period Grant gained a keen appreciation for Hancock's talents. "He commanded a corps longer than any other one, and his name was never mentioned as having committed in battle a blunder for which he was responsible," recalled Grant in his postwar memoirs. "His genial disposition made him friends, and his personal courage and his presence with his command in the thickest of the fight won for him the confidence of troops serving under him. No matter how hard the fight, the 2d corps always felt that their commander was looking after them."[1]

Hancock was involved in the early stages of the siege of Petersburg, Virginia, which began in mid-June 1864. However, health problems related to his wounds at Gettysburg once again flared up and forced Hancock from the front. After his return several weeks later, his corps was badly beaten by Confederate forces at the Second Battle of Reams' Station in August. In November he gave up command of the Second Corps, in part because his war wounds continued to bother him. He spent most of the remainder of the war engaged in recruiting, though he also briefly held command of Union forces in the Shenandoah Valley, which by this time had fallen under firm Federal control. On July 7, 1865, he supervised the execution of four Americans convicted of involvement in the April 14 assassination of President Abraham Lincoln by John

Wilkes Booth. On July 26, 1866, Hancock was promoted to major general in the regular U.S. Army.

## Remains in the Public Spotlight

Hancock became increasingly involved in American politics after the war. In 1867 he was appointed by President Andrew Johnson to oversee Reconstruction policies and programs in Texas and Louisiana. His reluctance to use U.S. military personnel to enforce new civil rights laws made him popular with white Southerners and Democrats who opposed Reconstruction, but his directorship was harshly criticized by Southern blacks and Republican political leaders.

In 1868 Hancock was removed from his position in the South by the new Republican administration of President Ulysses S. Grant. He was transferred west, to take command of military affairs in the Department of the Dakota. Hancock remained there until 1872, when he became commander of the Department of the Atlantic, with headquarters at Governor's Island in New York City. In 1880 Hancock won the Democratic nomination for the presidency, but he was narrowly defeated by Republican nominee James Garfield. He resumed his duties with the Department of the Atlantic, and he was still holding that office when he died on February 9, 1886, from complications associated with diabetes.

### Sources

Cluff, Mary Lynn. "Winfield Scott Hancock." In *Encyclopedia of the American Civil War: A Political, Social, and Military History.* David S. Heidler and Jeanne T. Heidler, eds. New York: W. W. Norton, 2000.
Jordan, David M. *Winfield Scott Hancock: A Soldier's Life.* Bloomington: Indiana University Press, 1988.
Tucker, Glenn. *Hancock the Superb.* Indianapolis: Bobbs-Merrill, 1960.

### Note

[1] Grant, Ulysses S. *Personal Memoirs of Ulysses S. Grant.* Volume 2. New York: C. L. Webster, 1885, pp. 539-40.

## Robert E. Lee (1807-1870)
*Confederate General of the Army of Northern Virginia*

Robert Edward Lee was born in Stratford Hall, Virginia, on January 19, 1807. He was the fourth child of Ann Hill Carter and Colonel Henry "Light-Horse Harry" Lee, a Revolutionary War hero and former governor of Virginia. Henry Lee's economic fortunes paled in comparison to his military and political exploits, however. He invested in several land speculation schemes that ended in failure, and his debts became so great that he fled to the West Indies, leaving his wife and six children behind. The disgraceful circumstances of his father's absence turned Robert E. Lee into a young man who placed a high value on self-control, duty, and sacrifice.

Unable to afford tuition at any of Virginia's finest universities, Lee enrolled in the U.S. Military Academy at West Point in 1825. He graduated second in his class in 1829. Two years later he married Mary Anna Randolph Custis, a wealthy great-granddaughter of America's first First Lady, Martha Washington. Their union brought Lee considerable prestige and wealth, for his wife's inheritance included huge tracts of prime Virginia real estate, nearly 200 slaves, and a fine plantation house outside Arlington, Virginia. They eventually had seven children together. Lee prized his family, but his military career took him away from his wife and children for months at a time. These separations, combined with Mary's poor health, at times put a heavy strain on their marriage.

## A Career Soldier

From 1829 to 1846 Lee served his country in the U.S. Army Corps of Engineers. For much of this time he was heavily involved in construction projects to improve harbors and rivers for commercial use and coastal defense. Lee's first battlefield experiences came in the Mexican War (1846-48), during which time he served as a key member of the staff of General Winfield Scott. By the time the war was over, Lee had been promoted to the rank of colonel and earned high marks from Scott and other military leaders.

In 1852 Lee was appointed superintendent of the West Point Military Academy. During the next few years he became acquainted with many young cadets who would become Union and Confederate officers in the Civil War. In 1855 Lee left West Point to become a cavalry commander at a post in Texas. He spent the next two years protecting white settlers from Indian war parties. In 1857, however, the death of Lee's father-in-law revealed that the family's plantations and other financial holdings had been poorly managed for many years. Lee had to take several leaves of absence to settle problems with the estate and return the family's various planting operations to good health.

In October 1859 Lee was ordered to respond to a raid on a federal armory at Harper's Ferry, Virginia. This raid had been led by radical abolitionist John Brown, who hoped that seizure of the armory might spark a major slave rebellion. Lee and the troops under his command captured Brown and his followers after a fierce but brief fight.

## Lee Sides with Virginia

The onset of the Civil War deeply saddened Lee, who had devoted his life to the U.S. military. For the Virginian, however, there was never any question for which side he would fight. His foremost allegiance was to his home state, and he faulted abolitionists for the sectional tensions that had brought North and South to blows. Lee was also a slaveholder himself, and his occasional expressions of personal discomfort with slavery never grew to the point of active opposition to the pro-slavery policies of the Confederacy.

Spurning an offer from the Lincoln administration to command the entire Union army, Lee submitted his resignation to the War Department on April 20. He then accepted command of the military and naval forces of Virginia, which days earlier had approved secession from the United States. Lee spent the first few months of the war in the field before being called to the Confederate capital of Richmond, Virginia, to serve as chief military advisor to President Jefferson Davis. He served in this capacity until May 1862, when he succeeded the wounded Joseph E. Johnston as general of the Army of Northern Virginia, the Confederacy's largest army.

Lee's first months leading the Army of Northern Virginia yielded mixed results. He skillfully repulsed an invasion of Virginia by the Union's Army of the Potomac in the so-called Seven Days' Battles of June 25-July 1. Lee was also victorious at the Second Battle of Bull Run (also known as Second Manassas) in Manassas, Virginia, in August 1862. His decision to take his army north of the Potomac

River into Maryland, however, resulted in the epic Battle of Sharpsburg, known in the North as the Battle of Antietam. This battle produced the highest one-day casualties of any Civil War battle (about 23,000 casualties combined between the two armies), and it forced Lee to withdraw back into Confederate territory.

## Battlefield Victories Make Lee a Beloved Figure

Back in Virginia Lee quickly put the bloody stalemate at Antietam behind him. In December 1862 Lee and the Army of Northern Virginia stamped out a Union offensive at the Battle of Fredericksburg. This triumph further cemented the reputation of Lee and his inner circle of generals as the pride of the Confederacy. "The Army of Northern Virginia [became] the most famous and successful of the Confederate armies," summarized the Civil War Trust. "This same organization … boasted some of the Confederacy's most inspiring military figures, including James Longstreet, Stonewall Jackson, and the flamboyant cavalier Jeb Stuart. With these trusted subordinates, Lee commanded troops that continually manhandled their blue-clad adversaries and embarrassed their generals no matter the odds."[1]

In early May 1863 Lee delivered his greatest victory of the war—an epic thrashing of Union general Joseph Hooker and his Army of the Potomac at Chancellorsville, Virginia. Hooker's invading army was twice the size of Lee's force, but the white-bearded Virginian tied Hooker into knots with a series of daring maneuvers. Dividing his army into three pieces, Lee repeatedly outflanked his enemy and leveled crushing attacks on the confused Federals.

By the time Hooker retreated back to the North, he had lost 17,000 men and the confidence of the Lincoln administration. By contrast, the Battle of Chancellorsville vaulted Lee to an exalted position in the minds of Confederate soldiers and Southern civilians alike. Many Confederates talked about the courtly Virginian with reverence that bordered on worship, and they expressed immense faith in Lee's abilities to defeat any Union army he confronted.

Lee shared his troops' high morale and confidence, but he recognized that Chancellorsville had been costly for the Army of Northern Virginia as well. Jackson was mortally wounded at Chancellorsville, and the battle had claimed 8,000 Confederate casualties. Since the pool of potential soldiers in the South was much smaller than in the North, Lee knew that the Army of Northern Virginia could only survive a limited number of such bloody engagements. With this in mind, Lee convinced Davis to approve another offensive into Northern territory. Lee's gamble was that if he could claim a big military victory on Northern soil, it might be enough to turn an already disillusioned Northern public firmly against the war. This would in turn give President Abraham Lincoln no choice but to give up his efforts to force the secessionist states back into the Union fold.

## A Crushing Setback at Gettysburg

Lee and the Army of Northern Virginia swept back into Union territory in June 1863, crossing the Potomac into Maryland and then Pennsylvania. The Army of the Potomac gave chase, and by June 28, when Lincoln replaced Hooker with General George G. Meade, both armies were drawing near to a little Pennsylvania town called Gettysburg. The battle between the two great armies began in earnest on the morning of July 1, and for the next three days they waged a grim struggle for victory.

Meade's army was concentrated in a defensive posture on a series of hills and ridges south of the town. Time and again, Lee pounded the enemy lines with artillery and infantry attacks, and on several occasions it appeared that the Union position might crumble. But the Federals held on each time, thanks in part to hesitant performances by a number of Lee's officers. On July 3 Lee ordered a final assault at the heart of the Union defenses arrayed before him, turning aside Longstreet's pleas to consider other strategies. This final assault, popularly known as Pickett's Charge, was a failure that produced huge casualties among the participating Confederate regiments. With his army deeply wounded, Lee had no choice but to withdraw back into Virginia.

After the war, Lee tried to minimize the impact of Gettysburg. In an 1868 letter to Major William M. McDonald of Virginia, Lee said that victory "would have been gained could one determined and united blow have been delivered by our whole line. As it was, victory trembled in the balance for three days, and the battle resulted in the infliction of as great an amount of injury as was received and in frustrating the Federal campaign for the season."[2] Civil War historians, however, believe that the Union triumph at Gettysburg, combined with the Federal victory at Vicksburg, Mississippi, on July 4, fundamentally shifted the war in favor of the Union.

## Lee Surrenders at Appomattox

Over the next twenty-one months, Lee and the Army of Northern Virginia waged a gritty struggle to ward off defeat. During that time, however, Union general Ulysses S. Grant kept relentless pressure on Lee. Aggressively using the Army of the Potomac and other Federal armies at his disposal, Grant absorbed occasional battlefield losses, secure in the knowledge that Lee's army was running out of soldiers, ammunition, horses, and food. By the summer of 1864 Lee was trapped defending Petersburg, a vital railroad artery for nearby Richmond.

In early April 1865 Lee and his army finally abandoned Petersburg and headed west in a desperate attempt to find food and link up with Confederate forces in North Carolina. They were quickly cut off by Grant's vastly superior forces, however. With the battered and hungry remnants of his army surrounded, Lee formally surrendered to Grant at Appomattox Court House in Virginia on April 9. Other Rebel armies still in the field quickly followed suit, and the Civil War finally drew to a close.

With the war over, Lee retired from military life. In October 1865 Lee accepted the presidency of Washington College (now Washington and Lee University) in Lexington, Virginia. He served in this position until his death in 1870. Historians say that his conciliatory remarks after the war about the need for peaceful reintegration into the Union were helpful in fostering a spirit of reconciliation between North and South. He also became a prominent supporter of establishing new schools to educate the South's newly free black population, but he opposed giving them voting rights. Lee's prewar family plantation, which had been seized by Union troops during the war, was turned into Arlington National Cemetery. Lee suffered a severe stroke on September 28, 1870, and he died in Lexington two weeks later, on October 12.

## Sources

Blount, Roy Jr. *Robert E. Lee.* Penguin Putnam: New York, 2003.

Carmichael, Peter S., ed. *Audacity Personified, the Generalship of Robert E. Lee.* Baton Rouge: Louisiana State University Press, 2004.

Freeman, Douglas Southall. *R. E. Lee: A Biography* (vols. I-IV). New York: Charles Scribner's Sons, 1935.

Gallagher, Gary W., ed. *Lee the Soldier.* Lincoln: University of Nebraska Press, 1999.

## Notes

[1] "Robert E. Lee, General." Civil War Trust, n.d. Retrieved from http://www.civilwar.org/education/history/biographies/robert-e-lee.html.

[2] Quoted in Lee, Robert Edward. *Recollections and Letters of General Robert E. Lee.* New York: Doubleday, 1904, p. 102.

## Abraham Lincoln (1809-1865)

*President of the United States during the Civil War, 1861-1865*

Abraham Lincoln was born in a log cabin near Hodgenville, Kentucky, on February 12, 1809. His pioneer parents were Thomas Lincoln and Nancy Hanks Lincoln, who also had two other children. Their first-born child was Abraham's older sister, Sarah. His younger brother, Thomas, died in infancy.

In 1817 the Lincoln family moved to Perry County, Indiana, where the family eked out a modest existence farming and hunting. Abraham's mother died two years after the move to Indiana, but his father married a widow, Sarah Bush Johnston, a few months later. Johnston had three children of her own, but biographers report that she developed a close emotional bond to young Abraham. She also tried to make up for his extremely limited schooling opportunities by encouraging him to explore literature. Lincoln was receptive to this message, and he became an avid reader.

In the spring of 1830 the Lincoln family relocated to Illinois. At this point the twenty-two-year-old Lincoln decided to strike out on his own. Tall, strong, and ambitious, he supported himself over the next several years in the small village of New Salem as a woodsplitter, postmaster, and shopkeeper. He also served as a captain of volunteer troops in the Black Hawk War, a conflict between white settlers and Native American tribes around Illinois and Michigan that raged for several months in 1832. Lincoln did not experience any actual battlefield action, however.

### Building a Political Career

Lincoln planted his first roots in the worlds of law and politics around this time. After several years of legal studies, he passed the state bar exam in 1837 and launched his career as an attorney. Lincoln also became active in the local Whig Party, which favored high taxes on foreign-made goods, heavy investment in new roads, schools, and other "internal improvements," and limited presidential powers. His first bid for a seat in the state senate in 1832 ended in defeat, but two years later he was elected to the state legislature. Lincoln ultimately served four successive terms in the Illinois House of Representatives from 1834 to 1842. During these years he was at times critical of slavery, but he also kept his distance from the abolitionist movement.

Lincoln's dual career as a legislator and lawyer led him to relocate to the state capital of Springfield, where in 1839 he met Mary Todd, the daughter of a wealthy slaveholding family from Lexington, Kentucky. Their courtship was a turbulent one, but they married in 1842 and eventually had four sons. Only one of these children, Robert, lived to adulthood.

In the mid-1840s Lincoln concentrated on his Springfield law practice, which he shared with William Herndon. He continued to spend the bulk of his time in the state capital, but he occasionally plied his trade at county courthouses across the state in order to supplement his income. In 1846 he won election to the U.S. House of Representatives as a Whig. He served in Washington for a single term (1847-1849), but his opposition to the Mexican-American War (1846-48) dimmed his popularity back home. Rather than go down to defeat in a re-election bid, Lincoln decided to return to his law practice in 1849.

Over the next few years, Lincoln further burnished his reputation as one of the most accomplished and successful attorneys in the state of Illinois. As the years passed, however, the young lawyer continued to follow the nation's turbulent political affairs—and especially the growing sectional tensions over slavery—with great interest.

The controversial Kansas-Nebraska Act of 1854 spurred Lincoln to return to the political arena. This legislation, which paved the way for the expansion of slavery into the nation's frontier West, outraged Lincoln. He publicly spoke out against the act, and in the process, he denounced slavery in harsher terms than ever before. Lincoln's Whig Party, meanwhile, became so bitterly divided over the Kansas-Nebraska Act and the larger issue of slavery that it fell apart. In 1856 Lincoln joined other Whigs from the Northern states in creating an antislavery Republican Party.

## Lincoln Versus Douglas

In 1857 the U.S. Supreme Court issued its infamous *Dred Scott* decision, which asserted that African Americans could never attain U.S. citizenship or enjoy any civil rights protections. The ruling disgusted Lincoln. He did not believe that blacks were intellectually or morally equal to whites, but he felt that

America's founding principles of life, liberty, and the pursuit of happiness should be extended to all men.

In early 1858 Lincoln decided to challenge U.S. senator Stephen Douglas, the architect of the Kansas-Nebraska Act, for his seat in Congress. The Republican Party formally endorsed his candidacy at a convention in which Lincoln delivered a famous assessment of the country's sectional tensions over slavery. "A house divided against itself cannot stand," he declared. "I believe this government cannot endure permanently half slave and half free. I do not expect the Union to be dissolved—I do not expect the house to fall—but I do expect it will cease to be divided. It will become all one thing, or all the other."

The 1858 Senate campaign between Lincoln and Douglas was one of the most famous in American political history. The two men battled each other in seven spirited one-on-one debates that were held all across Illinois before immense crowds. After the last debate concluded, state lawmakers in Illinois re-elected Douglas. Nevertheless, the eloquence and conviction displayed by Lincoln during the nationally publicized debates catapulted him to the forefront of the Republican Party's political leadership.

## Lincoln Wins the White House and the South Secedes

In May 1860 Lincoln received the Republican nomination for president of the United States. His vice presidential running mate was Hannibal Hamlin of Maine, a former Democrat. Lincoln's anti-slavery views made him enormously unpopular in the slaveholding South, but his path to the White House was greatly eased by dissension in the Democratic Party, which championed the institution of slavery and states' rights to permit slavery if they so wished. Democratic tensions increased to the point that its northern wing nominated one presidential candidate—Douglas—and southern Democrats nominated another politician—incumbent vice president John C. Breckinridge.

Douglas and Breckinridge ended up splitting the pro-slavery, anti-Lincoln vote on November 6, 1860. Lincoln was thus able to win the White House despite receiving only about 40 percent of the popular vote (a fourth candidate, Constitutional Union candidate John C. Bell, garnered a little more than 12 percent of the vote). Lincoln easily secured the necessary majority of electoral college votes, though, winning 180 out of the available 303 votes.

White Southerners viewed Lincoln's election victory as an unacceptable insult and threat to their way of life. Even before he was inaugurated in March

1861, seven Southern states announced their secession from the United States. By June, eleven Southern states had left the Union to form their own nation, the Confederate States of America.

## Fighting to Preserve the Union

Lincoln, though, refused to let the Southern states go. He believed that the South's secession—in response to election results that it simply did not like—was deeply immoral and unpatriotic. Lincoln also believed that as president of the United States, he had a profound obligation to preserve the Union, even if that meant war.

Lincoln spent the next four years overseeing the Union's military and political efforts to put down the Confederate rebellion and restore the Union. These were enormously difficult years for Lincoln, who was regularly condemned by political enemies as a foolish and ineffective leader. Lincoln himself privately expressed fears the war's rising toll of death and misery might eventually give him no choice but to let the Confederacy go its own way. He persevered, however, and as the war dragged on the president shifted the rationale for the war in a very important way.

On September 22, 1862, Lincoln issued the Emancipation Proclamation, which declared "that all persons held as slaves" in the Confederate states "are, and henceforward shall be free." Lincoln's statement also provided for the induction of African-American men into the Union Army and Union Navy. Many white Southerners dismissed the Proclamation, pointing out that Lincoln had no power to enforce the measure in the South. They missed the point, though. The Emancipation Proclamation made the Civil War not only a war to preserve the Union, but also to end the despicable practice of slavery. "It captured the hearts and imagination of millions of Americans and fundamentally transformed the character of the war," explained one historian. "After January 1, 1863 [when the Proclamation went into effect], every advance of federal troops expanded the domain of freedom."[1]

For the remainder of the war, Lincoln continued to frame the Northern cause as one of dedication to human liberty and preservation of the principles of America's Founding Fathers. He emphasized these themes on many occasions, including the dedication of the Soldiers' National Cemetery at Gettysburg, Pennsylvania, on November 19, 1863. In his famous address at Gettysburg, Lincoln vowed that "government of the people, by the people, for the people, shall not perish from the earth."

In late 1863 and 1864 Union armies registered a series of important military victories and moved ever deeper into Rebel territory. With the tide of the war finally turning in the North's favor, Lincoln was able to win re-election to a second presidential term in November 1864. By March 4, 1865, when Lincoln delivered his second inauguration speech, it was clear that the Confederacy could not stand much longer. Lincoln used the occasion to urge his countrymen to set aside bitterness and welcome their former countrymen back into the Union fold in the coming months. The most important goal in postwar America, he said, would be to "bind up the nation's wounds" and "achieve and cherish a just and lasting peace."

On April 9, Confederate general Robert E. Lee formally surrendered his army at Appomattox Court House, Virginia. Lee's surrender marked the final death blow to the Confederacy, and over the ensuing weeks the Southern states sullenly returned to the Union. Lincoln was not able to witness the restoration of the Union, however. Five days after the surrender at Appomattox, Lincoln was shot by a Confederate sympathizer, John Wilkes Booth, while attending a play in Washington, D.C. Lincoln died the following day. His violent death made it much more difficult for North and South to come back together in the decades following the war.

During his presidency, Lincoln was hated and despised in the North by his political enemies and in the South by its legions of white secessionists. Today, however, Lincoln is almost universally regarded as one of America's greatest presidents. Historians agree that were it not for his steadfast resolve and ability to transform the Civil War into a struggle for human liberty, the United States probably never would have been restored.

## Sources

Donald, David Herbert. *Lincoln.* New York: Simon and Schuster, 1996.

Foner, Eric. *The Fiery Trial: Abraham Lincoln and American Slavery.* New York: W. W. Norton, 2011.

Goodwin, Doris Kearns. *Team of Rivals: The Political Genius of Abraham Lincoln.* New York: Simon and Schuster, 2005.

McPherson, James M. *Tried by War: Abraham Lincoln as Commander in Chief.* New York: Penguin Press, 2008.

## Note

[1] "The Emancipation Proclamation." National Archives and Records Administration. n.d. Retrieved from http://www.archives.gov/exhibits/featured_documents/emancipation_proclamation/.

## James Longstreet (1821-1904)
*Confederate Corps Commander with the Army of Northern Virginia*

James "Pete" Longstreet was born in Edge-field District, South Carolina, on January 8, 1821. He was the third of five children born to James Longstreet Sr. and Mary Ann Dent, who owned a small cotton plantation in northeastern Georgia. At age nine James went to live in Augusta, Georgia, with his uncle, Augustus Baldwin Longstreet, who was a Methodist minister and newspaper editor. This arrangement was made so that the youngster could attend school at the Academy of Richmond County. In 1838 Longstreet gained entrance to the U.S. Military Academy at West Point in New York State. By the time he graduated in 1842, he had become friends with Ulysses S. Grant, George Pickett, George H. Thomas, William Rosecrans, and several other cadets who would become prominent Civil War generals. In 1848, in fact, Longstreet was part of Grant's wedding party—and some historians believe that he may have even been best man at the ceremony.

## Brings Battlefield Experience to the Confederate Army

Longstreet began his military career as a second lieutenant with the Fourth U.S. Infantry. He saw his first military combat in the Mexican-American War (1846-48), participating in major battles at Vera Cruz, Churubusco, and Chapultepec, where he was wounded in the thigh. During much of this time he fought side-by-side with Pickett, who would become one of Longstreet's most valued officers during the Civil War.

The decisive U.S. victory in the Mexican-American War greatly expanded America's territorial holdings in western North America. Once the war ended, Longstreet remained in the West, serving primarily in Texas and the New Mexico Territory. In 1848 he married Maria Louisa Garland, with whom he eventually had ten children.

Longstreet received promotions to captain in 1852 and major in 1858, but when the Civil War erupted in the spring of 1861 he reluctantly resigned from the U.S. Army and offered his services to the Confederate States of America. He began his life as a Confederate officer in July 1861 as a brigadier general under the command of P. G. T. Beauregard and then Joseph E. Johnston. Before the month was over Longstreet's brigade had turned back a Union advance at Blackburn's Ford, Virginia, and in October he and another fast-rising Confederate officer, Thomas "Stonewall" Jackson, were promoted to major general. Longstreet subsequently received command of a division of six brigades that would eventually become the foundation for the I Corps of the Army of Northern Virginia, the main Rebel army in the war's Eastern Theatre.

The winter of 1861-62 was a sorrow-filled one for Longstreet, who lost three of his children to a scarlet fever epidemic. By many accounts these losses changed Longstreet, who became more pensive and religious. Nonetheless, his command continued to display the professional characteristics for which Longstreet became well-known—strong attention to preparation, discipline, and training, both for officers and enlisted men.

Longstreet further burnished his reputation with his corps' strong performance at the May 5, 1862, Battle of Williamsburg, Virginia. Less than a month later, however, he was criticized for weak generalship at the Battle of Seven Pines (also known as the Battle of Fair Oaks), which ran from May 31 through June 1. Johnston was severely wounded in the battle, which ended in a draw. Confederate president Jefferson Davis eventually selected General Robert E. Lee to take command of Johnston's force, which soon became known as the Army of Northern Virginia.

## Lee's "Old War Horse"

Lee and Longstreet quickly struck up a personal rapport. Their bond was further strengthened when Longstreet showcased his cool demeanor and sophisticated sense of military tactics in major battles such as Second Bull Run, Antietam, and Fredericksburg, as well as numerous lesser skirmishes with Yankee forces. Lee began to affectionately refer to Longstreet as his "Old War Horse" and "the staff in my right hand."[1] In September 1862 Lee arranged promotions to lieutenant general for both Longstreet and Jackson. Lee also divided the Army of Northern Virginia into two corps headed by Longstreet and Jackson (Longstreet led I Corps, while Jackson commanded II Corps).

In the early spring of 1863 Lee sent Longstreet and two of his divisions into southern Virginia to replenish the army's food supplies. Longstreet did not return in time to take part in the May 1-4 Battle of Chancellorsville, which was perhaps Lee's single greatest battlefield victory of the entire war. He was able to rejoin Lee and the rest of the Army of Northern Virginia, however, for their bold June 1863 invasion into Maryland and Pennsylvania.

## Gettysburg Strains Longstreet's Relations with Lee

On July 1 Lee's Army of Northern Virginia met the Union's Army of the Potomac, commanded by General George G. Meade, in Gettysburg, Pennsylvania. Meade's forces managed to claim possession of a series of ridges and hills south of the town, but Lee tried again and again to cave in their defenses with waves of infantry assaults. As the bloody confrontation stretched on, Longstreet carefully but grimly conveyed his disapproval of Lee's tactics. He urged his commander to instead consider moving the Army of Northern Virginia around the far left flank of the Union defenses. Longstreet believed that such a maneuver would give Lee the option of either: 1) attacking any openings in Meade's defenses that presented themselves, or 2) advancing on Washington, D.C., which would force the Army of the Potomac to engage the Rebels on terrain that was less favorable to the Yankees. Lee rejected this advice, however.

On July 3 tensions between Longstreet and his commander escalated to new heights. Lee decided to launch a final major assault at the heart of the Union defenses at Gettysburg. Longstreet bluntly stated that the plan, which would require Lee's men to expose themselves to enemy fire in an open field for hundreds of yards, was doomed to failure. Once again, Lee rejected his subordinate's arguments. The attack commenced that afternoon, with troops from Longstreet's I Corps under Major General George Pickett leading the way. "Pickett's Charge" was turned aside by the Yankees, just as Longstreet had predicted. The assault resulted in staggering losses for the Army of Northern Virginia, as about half of the 12,000 Confederate soldiers involved in the action were either killed, wounded, or captured. This turn of events finally convinced Lee to withdraw from Gettysburg and return to Virginia.

In the fall of 1863 Longstreet and two of his I Corps divisions were sent to aid battered Confederate forces led by General Braxton Bragg in the West. Longstreet provided vital leadership at the September 19-20 Battle of Chickamauga in Georgia, which ended in a decisive victory for the South. That winter, though, relations between Bragg and Longstreet and their respective staffs became riddled with distrust and petty jealousies. Longstreet had been so dis-

150

illusioned by Gettysburg that he had received the order to head west with relief. By the spring of 1864, though, when he received new orders to return to Virginia, he was happy to leave Bragg and his crew behind.

Longstreet returned to Virginia in time to participate in the early phases of the Battle of the Wilderness, a series of clashes between the Army of Northern Virginia and Union general Ulysses S. Grant's Army of the Potomac that took place in May-June 1864. On May 6, though, Longstreet was accidentally shot by one of his own men. The wound left him with a permanently paralyzed right arm and kept him out of action until October 1864. By this time Lee and the rest of the Army of Northern Virginia were engaged in an ultimately hopeless effort to keep the Confederate capital of Richmond and nearby Petersburg, a vital rail center, out of Grant's hands. Lee finally abandoned Petersburg and Richmond in early April 1865, and on April 9 he surrendered the Army of Northern Virginia to Grant.

## Civil War Hero or Confederate Traitor?

Longstreet became an incredibly controversial figure among fellow Southerners after the war. He publicly endorsed Reconstruction policies that were enormously unpopular among white citizens. After Grant was elected president in 1868, Longstreet also accepted an offer from his old friend to serve in his administration as surveyor of customs for the Port of New Orleans and adjutant general of Louisiana's state militia. Longstreet's renewed association with Grant, who was both a Republican and the man who had forced Lee's surrender, further deepened feelings of hostility toward Longstreet across the Democrat-dominated South.

Longstreet's biggest sin, however, was to criticize Lee's wartime leadership—and in particular his decision making at Gettysburg—in his memoirs and in letters published in Louisiana newspapers. Jubal Early and other "Lost Cause" advocates responded to these criticisms of their beloved general with their own accusations that Longstreet had served Lee poorly at Gettysburg. Specifically, they alleged that Longstreet deliberately delayed the execution of critical orders on Day 2 and Day 3 at Gettysburg. Longstreet angrily denied these charges, but the Lost Causers succeeded in making him a villain in the eyes of multiple generations of white Southerners.

Modern historians, however, have generally praised Longstreet's wartime record. According to biographer Jeffry Wert, Longstreet "was the finest corps commander in the Army of Northern Virginia; in fact, he was arguably the best corps commander in the conflict on either side."[2] Civil War historian Stephen W. Sears echoed this sentiment. He wrote that "there is no doubt that Longstreet, exercising what he thought of as the prerogative of a corps commander, argued strongly against Lee's attack plans on the 2nd and 3rd. There is no doubt either that he directed those attacks with a heavy heart. Yet there is also no doubt that when he struck, he struck as hard as he always did.... At Gettysburg, James Longstreet was the only one of Lee's corps commanders who lived up to expectations."[3]

In 1874 politically fueled riots raged across New Orleans. When Longstreet tried to quell the riots through the use of a police force that included black officers, his reputation among white residents suffered yet another blow. He was scorned by former friends, and it became dangerous for him to walk the streets of the city. In 1875 Longstreet relocated his family to Gainesville, Georgia, where he established a small farm. In 1889 Longstreet lost his house and many personal papers from the Civil War era in a fire. Later that year, his wife, Louisa, passed away after forty-one years of marriage. In 1897 he married the much younger Helen Dortch. Longstreet died in Gainesville, Georgia, on January 2, 1904.

## Sources

Callihan, David L. "Neither Villain Nor Hero: A Reassessment of James Longstreet's Performance at Gettysburg." *The Gettysburg Magazine*, January 2002.

Connelly, Thomas L., and Barbara L. Bellows. *God and General Longstreet: The Lost Cause and the Southern Mind.* Baton Rouge: Louisiana State University Press, 1982.

Piston, William G. *Lee's Tarnished Lieutenant: James Longstreet and His Place in Southern History.* Athens: University of Georgia Press, 1990.

Wert, Jeffry D. *General James Longstreet: The Confederacy's Most Controversial Soldier: A Biography.* New York: Simon & Schuster, 1993.

Wert, Jeffry D. "James Longstreet: Robert E. Lee's Most Valuable Soldier." *Civil War Times,* August 2006. Retrieved from http://www.historynet.com/james-longstreet-robert-e-lees-most-valuable-soldier.htm.

## Notes

[1] Quoted in Wert, Jeffry D. "James Longstreet: Robert E. Lee's Most Valuable Soldier." *Civil War Times,* August 2006. Retrieved from http://www.historynet.com/james-longstreet-robert-e-lees-most-valuable-soldier.htm.

[2] Wert, Jeffry D. *General James Longstreet: The Confederacy's Most Controversial Soldier: A Biography.* New York: Simon & Schuster, 1993, p. 405.

[3] Sears, Stephen W. *Gettysburg.* Boston: Houghton Mifflin, 2003, pp. 503-4.

# George G. Meade (1815-1872)

*Union General Who Commanded the Army of the Potomac at Gettysburg*

George Gordon Meade was born in Cadiz, Spain, on New Year's Eve of 1815. He was the eighth of eleven children born to Richard W. Meade and Margaret Coats Butler Meade. Both of his parents were Americans, but his businessman father went to Spain to serve as a naval agent for the U.S. government. Richard Meade suffered severe financial setbacks during the Napoleonic Wars that swept across Europe in the early nineteenth century, and in 1828 he died. Facing the prospect of financial ruin in Spain, Margaret Meade took her children back to the United States and settled in Philadelphia, Pennsylvania.

In 1831 Meade entered the U.S. Military Academy at West Point, New York. After graduating in 1835 he spent a year in Florida fighting Seminole Indians as a member of the 3rd U.S. Artillery. Dissatisfied with military life, Meade then left the army behind to work as a civil engineer for a private railroad company. On his twenty-fifth birthday he married Margaretta Sergeant, with whom he eventually had seven children.

## Return to Army Life

In 1842 Meade decided that the army offered more financial stability than an engineering career in the private business world. His request to be reinstated into the U.S. Army was approved, and he was appointed a second lieutenant in the Corps of Topographical Engineers. He served during the Mexican-American War (1846-1848) as an officer on the staff of Major General Zachary Taylor during his successful (and brutal) invasion of northern Mexico.

After the Mexican-American War concluded, Meade spent the next decade supervising harbor improvements, designing lighthouses, and conducting topographic surveys along the East Coast and in the Great Lakes. These quiet but productive years of service provided no clues that Meade would one day be appointed commander of the largest Union army in the Civil War.

Meade's rapid ascent to that position began a few months after the Confederates' April 1861 attack on Fort Sumter, which marked the start of the Civil War. On August 31 Meade received a promotion from captain to brigadier general of volunteers and took command of a brigade of Pennsylvania reserves. He and his men spent the next several months aiding in the construction of defenses around Washington, D.C. In the spring of 1862, Meade's brigade marched with Major General George B. McClellan's Army of the Potomac into Virginia. The goal of this so-called Peninsular Campaign, which ran from March to July 1862, was to capture the Confederate capital of Richmond. McClellan was turned back, though, by Confederate general Robert E. Lee and his Army of Northern Virginia.

Meade suffered several serious wounds during the Seven Days' Battles segment of the Peninsular Campaign, but he recovered in time to lead his brigade at the Second Battle of Bull Run in August 1862. Meade then was named a divisional commander in the Army of the Potomac's I Corps, which was headed by Joseph Hooker. Meade led his troops with decisiveness and vigor at the September 14 Battle of South Mountain, a clash for control of Appalachian passes that Lee was using to invade Maryland. Three days later the armies met at the bloody Battle of Antietam near Sharpsburg, Maryland. Meade replaced the wounded Hooker as commander of I Corps during the battle, and by the time the bloodshed had ceased Meade had been wounded again.

## Taking the Reins of the Army of the Potomac

Meade returned to division command, and he performed ably in that capacity at two major battles—Fredericksburg and Chancellorsville—that rocked the Army of the Potomac to its core. In recognition of his division's strong performance at Fredericksburg in December 1862, Meade was promoted to major general. The loss at Fredericksburg also led to Hooker's promotion to generalship of the entire Army of the Potomac.

The humiliating defeat at Chancellorsville in the spring of 1863, however, cost Hooker his command. He was relieved on June 28 while the Army of the Potomac was in the midst of pursuing Lee and his Army of Northern Virginia through southern Pennsylvania. President Abraham Lincoln's first choice to replace Hooker had been Major General John F. Reynolds. But Reynolds declined when he was told that he would have to devise wartime strategies in regular consultation with War Department officials like General-in-Chief Henry Halleck and War Secretary Edwin M. Stanton. Lincoln subsequently extended the reins of the Army of the Potomac to Meade, who took over on June 28.

Meade had taken command of the Union army just as it was drawing near to Lee and his invading force. The two armies finally met at the small town of Gettysburg on the morning of July 1, 1863, and for three solid days the south-central Pennsylvania countryside echoed with the roar of artillery shells, rifle fire, screaming horses, and groaning men. Meade and his top officers managed to hold their defensive positions throughout the bloody contest. A failed Confederate offensive on Day Three left Lee's army in such poor shape that the Confederate general was forced to order a retreat back to Virginia.

Flooding along the Potomac River delayed Lee's retreat for several days, but Meade decided against launching a major attack that might shatter the Army of Northern Virginia. He thought that his own army had absorbed too much punishment. Meade's decision not to move against Lee's weakened forces angered and frustrated Lincoln, who felt that the general let a golden opportunity to destroy the Confederacy's main army slip away. Meade submitted his resignation to the president, but it was denied, and he received a promotion to brigadier general in the regular army on July 7.

## Making Way for Grant

Meade and Lee clashed on a few more occasions in the fall and winter of 1863, but Meade's caution in the face of Lee's strong defensive posture kept any major battles from erupting. In March 1864 Lincoln appointed Ulysses S. Grant as general-in-chief over all Union forces. Grant decided to travel with the Army of the Potomac instead of directing affairs from Washington as Halleck had done. When Meade learned about this development, he again offered his resignation, explaining that Grant should have the right to have an officer of his own choosing at the head of the Army of the Potomac. Grant refused the offer, and he later indicated that Meade's dignity and selflessness greatly impressed him.

Meade remained the official commander of the Army of the Potomac for the remainder of the Civil War. In reality, though, Grant made all the big decisions about how the army and its various components were used. For example, Grant greatly expanded the use of the army's cavalry as a combat force. Meade initially disapproved of this decision, but it proved to be very beneficial to the Federal cause during the war's final months.

During the course of 1864 and early 1865 Grant and Meade worked together against Lee at several significant battles, including the Wilderness Campaign, Spotsylvania, and Cold Harbor. They also collaborated on the Siege of

Petersburg, which greatly drained Lee's Army of Northern Virginia. In each of these instances, Grant made the major command decisions, while Meade was responsible for giving the specific orders necessary to carry out Grant's wishes. In August 1864 Grant arranged for Meade to be promoted to major general, a clear indication that he appreciated Meade's professionalism and steadiness.

On April 9, 1865, Lee finally surrendered to Grant at Appomattox Court House, Virginia. Meade was not present for this event, which seemed to symbolize how he had come to be overshadowed by Grant. Meade remained in the army after the war, serving as a military commander of Federal forces in the South during Reconstruction. He also served as a commissioner of Philadelphia's Fairmount Park. He died in his adopted home town of Philadelphia on November 6, 1872. His death was attributed to a combination of pneumonia and continued health complications from old war wounds.

## Sources

Cleaves, Freeman. *Meade of Gettysburg.* Norman: University of Oklahoma Press, 1991.
Trudeau, Noah Andre. *Gettysburg: A Testing of Courage.* New York: HarperCollins, 2002.

## George E. Pickett (1825-1875)
*Confederate General Who Led Pickett's Charge
at Gettysburg*

George Edward Pickett was born in Richmond, Virginia, on January 16, 1825. He was the oldest of eight children born to Robert and Mary Pickett, who had ancestral ties to Virginia's first settlers. In 1842 he entered the U.S. Military Academy at West Point, New York, where he became better known for his pranks and carefree manner than his studies. Pickett's indifference to his studies was reflected in his class ranking; he finished dead last among the 59 cadets who graduated from West Point in 1846. Nonetheless, he did manage to graduate, after which he received a commission as a brevet second lieutenant in the U.S. Eighth Infantry Regiment.

### From Mexico to Washington Territory

The timing of Pickett's graduation thrust him into the thick of the Mexican-American War (1846-48). He had his first moment of military glory in the September 1847 Battle of Chapultepec, a key victory for the U.S. Army in its successful invasion of Mexico. During the American assault on Chapultepec Castle, Pickett's friend and fellow officer, James Longstreet, was wounded while carrying their regiment's flag, or "colors." Longstreet handed over the colors to Pickett, who rocketed to the roof of the castle. He then waved the flag to and fro as the castle's Mexican defenders surrendered. By the time the Mexican-American War ended, Pickett had earned a brevet promotion to captain.

After the war Pickett was posted to the Texas frontier, where he gradually rose through the ranks. He was promoted to first lieutenant in 1849 and captain in 1855. In January 1851 Pickett married Sally Harrison Minge, a distant relative of the late president William Henry Harrison. Their union lasted less than a year, though, as she died during childbirth in November.

In the mid-1850s Pickett was sent to the Washington Territory, where he supervised the building of Fort Bellingham. During his posting there he married a local Haida Indian, but she died shortly after giving birth to a son. Pickett cared for the boy, James, for the next four years, but he left him in the care of friends in the territory when the Civil War began. He knew that his mixed-race son would never be accepted in the South. Pickett never again saw his son, who would later became a well-known regional artist.

In 1859 Pickett found himself in the center of a strange but potentially dangerous dispute called the Pig War with British military forces in Washington's San Juan Islands. The conflict centered on whether the British had the right to arrest and prosecute an American farmer who had killed a bothersome hog belonging to the powerful Hudson's Bay Trading Company, which was British-owned. Pickett and a contingent of American soldiers were sent to the islands to defend the farmer—and by extension, American sovereignty over the islands. British warships subsequently patrolled the islands in menacing fashion, but their captains avoided a full-blown confrontation with Pickett. Tensions gradually eased, and the dispute was eventually solved through diplomatic channels.

## A Confederate Officer with Anti-Slavery Views

When Virginia seceded from the Union in April 1861 to join the Confederacy, Pickett immediately resigned from the U.S. Army—despite the fact that he saw slavery as a deeply immoral institution. He was given the rank of colonel in the Confederate military and spent the fall of 1861 overseeing the defense of Virginia's lower Rappahannock River. In January 1862 he was promoted to brigadier general.

Pickett saw extensive combat during the spring 1862 Peninsular Campaign, a Union offensive into Virginia conducted by General George McClellan and his Army of the Potomac. Serving under his old friend and comrade Longstreet, Pickett led his brigade into battle at three of the so-called Seven Days' Battles (Williamsburg, Seven Pines, and Gaines' Mill) during that campaign. Pickett was shot in the shoulder at Gaines' Mill, and he spent the summer recovering. When he resumed active duty in the fall, he returned to Longstreet's side, this time as a major general in Longstreet's I Corps of the Army of Northern Virginia.

Pickett's division was not heavily involved in the December 1862 Battle of Fredericksburg, which ended in a decisive victory for the Army of Northern Virginia and its commander, Robert E. Lee. In the spring of 1863 Lee sent Longstreet and two of his divisions—including Pickett's—on a resupply mission into southern Virginia. As a result, Pickett missed the Battle of Chancellorsville (May 1-4), which ranks as Lee's best-known triumph of the entire war. Pickett expressed enormous frustration about missing out on the action at Fredericksburg and Chancellorsville, and he openly pined for an opportunity to lead his division into a major battle.

## Pickett's Disastrous Charge at Gettysburg

In June 1863 Lee led the Army of Northern Virginia into Pennsylvania for the purpose of replenishing supplies from area farms, threatening Northern cities, and possibly winning a battle or two that would end the war in the Confederacy's favor. As Lee moved toward the town of Gettysburg he assigned Pickett's division to guard supply and communication lines at the rear of his army. As a result, Pickett did not reach the battlefield at Gettysburg until the night of July 2, by which time the Army of Northern Virginia had already engaged in two days of fierce combat with the Union's Army of the Potomac.

On July 3, Pickett's division of fresh infantry troops was selected to lead a Confederate assault aimed at the heart of the Union defenses. Pickett's division would be supplemented by six brigades under the direction of Brigadier General J. Johnston Pettigrew and Major General Isaac R. Trimble. Lee believed that if the troops commanded by Pickett, Pettigrew, and Trimble could traverse an open field and reach the high ground where the Yankees had established their lines, they could break the battlefield stalemate and claim a smashing victory.

Pickett was thrilled by the assignment. The attack, though, proved to be a complete disaster for his division and the Army of Northern Virginia. Union rifles and artillery carved up the exposed Confederates without mercy as they crossed open terrain, and the surviving remnants of the Pickett-Pettigrew-Trimble units were too weak to break the enemy's defenses. By the time Pickett's Charge, as it came to be known, was over and the Rebel troops had retreated, about half of the 12,000 troops who participated in the assault had been slain, wounded, or captured. The shocking casualty count forced Lee to withdraw from Gettysburg and return to Virginia. Pickett survived the charge without sustaining injury, but he was grief-stricken about the heavy losses incurred by his division. According to some Confederates who served with Pickett, he remained embittered about Lee's decision to order the July 3 charge for the rest of his life.

On November 13, 1863, Pickett married Sallie Ann Corbell, with whom he eventually had two sons. He also was reassigned to lead the Department of Southern Virginia and North Carolina. In the spring of 1864 he began reporting to General P. G. T. Beauregard, who was responsible for the defenses around Richmond, which was both the capital of the Confederacy and Pickett's native city. When Union forces under General Ulysses S. Grant invaded Virginia in the Overland Campaign, Pickett's division was sent to help Lee ward off the invaders. The Union armies proved too strong, however, and by late summer the Army of Northern Virginia had been cornered into a defensive posture around Petersburg, a vital supply line for Richmond.

On April 1, 1865, Pickett's troops were soundly beaten at the Battle of Five Forks by Union forces under General Philip Sheridan. This defeat cast a shadow over Pickett's reputation, as he was attending a fish bake two miles away from the battlefield when Sheridan struck. Some military records indicate that Lee may have stripped Pickett of his command as a result of Five Forks, but historians differ on the likelihood of this. In any event, the loss of Five Forks cut off the last Confederate railroad supply line into Petersburg. When Lee heard this news, he evacuated his dwindling army out of Petersburg and made a desperate dash to the west to escape being crushed by Grant. Union forces quickly surrounded him, though, and on April 9 Lee formally surrendered to Grant, bringing the Civil War to a close. Pickett surrendered with his men—an indication that if Lee did issue orders relieving him of command, he never received them.

After the war Pickett worked as an insurance agent. Like many other West Pointers who served in the Confederate Army, he eventually received a full pardon from the U.S. government for his Civil War activities. He died in Norfolk, Virginia, on July 30, 1875. After his death, several romanticized books about his life were written and published by his widow, Sallie.

## Sources

Gordon, Lesley J. *General George E. Pickett in Life and Legend*. Chapel Hill: University of North Carolina Press, 1998.

Longacre, Edward G. *Pickett, Leader of the Charge: A Biography of General George E. Pickett, C.S.A.* Shippensburg, PA: White Mane Publishing, 1995.

## J. E. B. "Jeb" Stuart (1833-1864)
*Confederate Cavalry Officer with the Army of Northern Virginia*

James Ewell Brown Stuart, better known as "Jeb" for most of his life, was born on February 6, 1833, in Patrick County, Virginia. Stuart's family lineage was a proud military one. His great grandfather had served as a regimental commander for the colonists during the Revolutionary War, and his father, Archibald Stuart, had served in the War of 1812 before going on to become a plantation owner and U.S. congressman.

Stuart attended Emory and Henry College in Emory, Virginia, before enrolling at the U.S. Military Academy at West Point, New York. He graduated near the top of his class in 1854. In 1855 he married Flora Cook, with whom he had two daughters (one died on the same day she was born). By all accounts, Stuart was extremely devoted to his wife and family. After leaving West Point Stuart entered the U.S. Army as a second lieutenant (he was promoted to first lieutenant in 1855) in the cavalry. He spent the next several years fighting Apache Indians in Texas and serving at forts scattered across the Kansas Territory. During this time he gained a reputation as one of the more promising young cavalry officers in the West.

In October 1859 Stuart volunteered as an aide to Robert E. Lee (his former superintendent at West Point), who at the time was preparing to confront abolitionist John Brown and his followers after their raid on a federal armory at Harper's Ferry, Virginia. Stuart accompanied Lee to Harper's Ferry, where U.S. Marines under Lee's command captured Brown and his men after a brief struggle.

### The Confederacy's Dashing Cavalier

On April 22, 1861, Stuart was promoted to captain in the U.S. Army. When he learned that his home state of Virginia had seceded, however, the cavalryman submitted his resignation on May 3, 1861. One week later, he accepted a commission as a lieutenant colonel in the fast-forming Confederate army.

Stuart reported to Thomas "Stonewall" Jackson, who assigned him to command cavalry units of Joseph E. Johnston's Army of the Shenandoah in Virginia. These companies were quickly consolidated into the First Virginia Cavalry, with Stuart at its head. On July 21—five days after being promoted to colonel—Stuart's cavalry operations helped the Confederates to a smashing victory at the First Battle of Manassas, the first major engagement of the Civil War. Stuart was promoted to brigadier general in September 1861, and in March 1862 he was given command of all cavalry brigades for the Army of Northern Virginia (which had been cobbled together out of the Army of the Shenandoah and other Confederate forces).

Stuart's value to the Confederacy—and his reputation as a flamboyant and fearless cavalry officer—was firmly established in the spring of 1862, when the Army of Northern Virginia repulsed the so-called Peninsular Campaign of Union general George B. McClellan and his Army of the Potomac. Stuart led 1,200 Confederate cavalry in a three-day "Ride Around McClellan" that yielded vital intelligence about the enemy's strength and movements. This information enabled Lee, who by this time had assumed command of the Army of Northern Virginia, to craft the strategy that ultimately pushed McClellan out of Virginia.

Stuart continued to lead Lee's cavalry units throughout the remainder of 1862. The colorful cavalry commander was thus heavily involved in major clashes with enemy forces at the Second Battle of Manassas (August 29-30), the Battle of Antietam (September 17), and the Battle of Fredericksburg (December 13). After each battle, Lee expressed appreciation for the high quality of Stuart's scouting reports and his leadership in combat.

## Chancellorsville and Gettysburg

Stuart further burnished his reputation at the Battle of Chancellorsville, which raged from May 1 to May 4, 1863. A key turning point of the battle came when Stuart's cavalry discovered that the Army of the Potomac's right flank was exposed. This information enabled Jackson to deliver a punishing blow that caved in the entire right side of the enemy position and forced Union general Joseph Hooker to order a humiliating retreat. Stuart also temporarily took command of Jackson's men at Chancellorsville after Jackson was mortally wounded.

The triumph at Chancellorsville was overshadowed two months later, however, by events in Pennsylvania. When Lee decided to take the Army of Northern Virginia into the North in June 1863, Stuart and his 9,500-man cavalry rode at the forefront of that campaign. Before Stuart even left Virginia, though, he was surprised in a pre-dawn raid by a large Union assault force led by General Alfred Pleasonton. Stuart quickly rallied his horsemen, but unlike every previous clash of cavalry in the war, the Confederates were unable to bend the enemy to their will. Instead, the Yankee cavalry fought them to a bloody draw at what came to be known as the Battle of Brandy Station.

Stuart was embarrassed by the whole Brandy Station mess. As the Army of Northern Virginia passed over the Potomac River and onto Northern soil, he coaxed Lee into allowing him to conduct cavalry raids to the east. Lee grudgingly approved the plan, which many historians attribute to Stuart's desire to wash away the unpleasant memory of Brandy Station. But Lee emphasized to Stuart that the primary duty of his cavalry was unchanged: to provide timely reports on Union troop movements and screen the rest of Lee's army from enemy observation.

Stuart failed to fulfill these commitments. He departed from Lee's side on the morning of June 25 with his three best brigades. After conducting a number of raids to the east, though, he found that his route back to Lee had been cut off by the Army of the Potomac, which was hot on the Army of Northern Virginia's trail. As a result, he and his men had to take a long and circuitous route to get back to Lee's army. Stuart's progress was further slowed by his decision to travel with more than 100 Union supply wagons he had captured. Meanwhile, Lee and the Army of Northern Virginia kept moving deeper into enemy territory without any information from Stuart's cavalry about enemy strength or movements. As a result, Lee and his army became unintentionally drawn into a full-blown clash with the Army of the Potomac at Gettysburg, Pennsylvania. Stuart was unable to rejoin Lee until the evening of July 2, by which time the Battle of Gettysburg had been raging for two days.

On the third and final day of battle at Gettysburg, Lee sent Stuart and a large contingent of cavalry south of the Union lines in an effort to distract the enemy from the main Confederate assault directed at Yankee forces arrayed along Cemetery Ridge. But Stuart's hopes to make up for his long absence were dashed by Union cavalry units that battled him to a draw. Meanwhile, Lee's final infantry assault, known as Pickett's Charge, ended in failure. On July 4 the battered Army of Northern Virginia withdrew from Gettysburg and began the long trek back to Virginia.

In the months and years since that pivotal battle, Stuart's disappearance in the days leading up to the meeting with the Army of the Potomac has been cited as a key factor in the Confederate loss. Defenders of Stuart have pointed out, however, that Lee was not totally without cavalry in the days leading up to Gettysburg. They argue that Lee could have found out more about the enemy's whereabouts if he had made more aggressive use of the cavalry brigades that Stuart left behind.

## Stuart's Last Days

In May 1864 Union general Ulysses S. Grant brought the Army of the Potomac back into Virginia in his so-called Overland Campaign, which was based on the idea that shattering Lee's army would break the back of the Confederacy once and for all. Stuart and his cavalry performed admirably during several early clashes, including the Battle of the Wilderness (May 5-7) and the early stages of the Battle of Spotsylvania (May 8-21). On May 11, though, Stuart was mortally wounded at the Battle of Yellow Tavern, a fierce engagement with Union horsemen under the command of General Philip Sheridan. The battle took place only six miles north of Richmond, the Confederate capital, so aides were able to take Stuart into the city for medical care. On May 12, though, Stuart died of his wounds.

After the war Stuart remained one of the most popular of the Confederate generals in white Southern culture. He benefited greatly from the Lost Cause movement's decision to place the blame for the loss at Gettysburg at the feet of James Longstreet, Lee's senior corps commander. In fact, the dashing Stuart became a leading symbol of the Lost Cause, ranking behind only Lee and Jackson in that movement's postwar mythology.

### Sources

Thomas, Emory M. *Bold Dragoon: The Life of J. E. B. Stuart*. New York: Harper and Row, 1986.

Wert, Jeffry D. *Cavalryman of the Lost Cause: A Biography of J. E. B. Stuart*. New York: Simon and Schuster, 2009.

Wittenberg, Eric J., and J. David Petruzzi. *Plenty of Blame to Go Around: Jeb Stuart's Controversial Ride to Gettysburg*. El Dorado Hills, CA: Savas Beatie, 2006.

# PRIMARY SOURCES

# The Army of Northern Virginia Invades Pennsylvania

*When Confederate general Robert E. Lee and his Army of Northern Virginia entered Pennsylvania in June 1863, civilian residents of the towns through which they passed were helpless to stop them. In Chambersburg, for example, townspeople accepted that they had no choice but to endure the temporary Rebel occupation. One Chambersburg resident, merchant Jacob Hoke, even took the opportunity to write an account of the event. In the following passage from his memoir, Hoke describes the appearance and attitude of the enemy troops. He also relates a conversation between several Confederate officers and H. E. Hoke, one of the author's own relatives. Hoke matter-of-factly tells the officers that they are doomed to lose, given the North's huge advantage in manpower.*

## Thursday, [June] 25th.

On this, as on the day previous, infantry, artillery and long trains of wagons passed through town and on down towards Harrisburg. As already stated the corps of Hill and Longstreet crossed the Potomac on the day previous—Wednesday, 24th. It will thus be seen that the army which was moving into our State extended from the Potomac to Shippensburg, a distance of forty miles....

First, as is usually the case with armies on the march, came a brigade of cavalry, and after an interval, the different regiments and brigades composing a division. There were here and there along the line bands of excellent music. "Dixie" and "My Maryland" were the favorite pieces played. These were followed by a train of artillery composed of cannon, caissons, and forges; then a long train of heavily loaded wagons, filled with shot, shells, and other ammunition. These wagons were each drawn by four or six horses or mules, and in passing through our streets they made that grinding noise which indicated immense weight of freightage. The wagon train was usually followed by another train of reserve artillery and from fifty to one hundred cattle for the use of the division. Following this division, after a short interval, came another, and another, in the same order, until an entire corps had passed.... Many of the wagons, horses, mules, and cannon bore the inscription "U.S.," and were evidently captured or stolen from the government....

The rebel infantry, as they marched through our streets, presented a solid front. They came in close marching order, the different brigades, divisions, and corps, all within supporting distance. Their dress consisted of nearly every imaginable style and color, the butternut largely predominating. Some had blue blouses, which they had captured, or stripped from the Union dead. Hats, or the skeletons of what were once hats, surmounted their partly covered heads.

167

Many were ragged, dirty and shoeless, affording unmistakable evidence that they sadly stood in need of having their wardrobes replenished. They were all, however, well armed and under perfect discipline. They seemed to move as one vast machine, and laughing, talking, singing, or cheering, was not indulged in. Straggling was scarcely seen, but when any did wander away from the lines, and find any of our citizens in retired places while they occupied the town, they did not hesitate to appropriate to themselves hats, boots, watches, and pocket books. This proves that their good behavior when under the eyes of their officers was due to discipline rather than innate honesty or good breeding....

The officers in command of the infantry like the men composing the cavalry, were of the higher and better class. Many of them with whom we had business transactions seemed to be perfect gentlemen, and while compelled to appropriate to the use of their army our property, to be paid for in worthless scrip, they did it in an apologizing way. Some of them were overheard to express their fears that they had run into a trip by coming over into our State, but the usual remark was, "Uncle Robert has brought us here, and he will see us out all right." In looking upon the large number of persons who gathered into the town on Sunday to see them, some of the rebels inquired if they were not soldiers in disguise. When answered that they were not, and the population and resources of the North were not yet scarcely touched, they seemed greatly astonished.

A case of this kind occurred one morning in front of the residence of Mr. H. E. Hoke, on East Market street. Imboden's cavalry had came in the evening previous and some of the officers were sitting on the steps of Mr. Hoke's residence, their horses being hitched to the shade trees. Upon Mr. Hoke's appearance one of the officers, apparently one of considerable rank, thus addressed him, "How long is this war going to last?" He replied, "You can answer that question better than I can." "What do you mean by that?" inquired the officer. "I mean that this war will last as long as you in the South are able to fight. If you can stand it twenty years more, then the war will last twenty years yet." The officer was evidently impressed, which emboldened Mr. Hoke to say further: "You must have seen for yourselves since you have come North that there are any number of able-bodied men yet to draw on, and the people of the North have scarcely awakened to the fact that there is a war on their hands, but this invasion will stir them up, and if it were possible for you to annihilate the whole of our armies now in the field, that would only bring out another to take you some morning for breakfast." They all listened in silence, and seemed to be thunderstruck, when one, who was lying on the cellar door, said with an oath, "There is more truth than fun in what he says." ...

It was a subject of frequent remark by the rebels about the magnificent country and large and flourishing towns they had seen since coming north. The dwelling houses of the farmers and the large and excellent barns also excited their admiration and astonishment. Letters written while here to be sent to their friends in the South, but lost from their pockets, were picked up on the streets. In some of these their expressions of astonishment at the rich and beautiful country, the excellent farming and fine large houses and barns, were profuse and decided....

*[The Confederate occupation of Chambersburg continues over the next several days, during which time the rebel army confiscates supplies from the surrounding countryside and destroys the local railroad.]*

## Monday, June 29th.

On the evening of this day, some time after dark, the writer, in company with Mr. H. E. Hoke and Mr. George R. Colliflower, went up into the steeple of the Reformed church. From that elevated position we had an uninterrupted view for miles all about us. The line of the railroad could be traced south of the town by the numerous fires still burning. The sound of the drum was heard from Pickett's camp about two miles southward. Along the South Mountain for miles up and down the valley innumerable strange lights were seen flashing to and fro. That these lights were used as signals for communication information, we well knew, but their occasion and import we were of course ignorant of.... Some time in the after part of that night, probably about two o'clock in the morning, I was awakened by my wife, who told me that some important movement was going on among the Confederates and that I should get up and come to the window. Peering cautiously through the half-closed shutters we saw a continuous stream of wagons driven hurriedly through the street. They were coming back from the direction of Harrisburg and passing up Main Street to the Diamond, turned east towards Gettysburg. The wagons were driven at a rapid pace, sometimes at a fast trot. They seemed to be heavily laden and caused a grinding noise upon the pike as they passed along.

They proved to be Ewell's train, and contained ammunition for the great battle then near at hand....

## Source

Hoke, Jacob. *Historical Reminiscences of the War: Or, Incidents Which Transpired in and about Chambersburg during the War of the Rebellion*. Chambersburg, PA: M. A. Foltz, 1884, pp. 54-55, 67.

# Lee's Army Advances to Gettysburg

*In the following excerpt from Robert E. Lee's Civil War memoirs, the Confederate commander of the Army of Northern Virginia gave his perspective on how the first day of the Battle of Gettysburg unfolded.*

The advance against Harrisburg was arrested by intelligence received from a scout on the night of the 28th [of June] to the effect that the army of General [Joseph] Hooker had crossed the Potomac and was approaching the South Mountains. In the absence of the cavalry it was impossible to ascertain his intentions; but to deter him from advancing farther west and intercepting our communications with Virginia it was determined to concentrate the army east of the mountains.

## Battle of Gettysburg

[A. P.] Hill's corps was accordingly ordered to move toward Cashtown on the 29th, and [James] Longstreet to follow the next day, leaving [George] Pickett's division at Chambersburg to guard the rear until relieved by [John D.] Imboden. General [Richard] Ewell was recalled from Carlisle, and directed to join the army at Cashtown or Gettysburg as circumstances might require. The advance of the enemy to the latter place was unknown, and the weather being inclement the march was conducted with a view to the comfort of the troops. [Henry] Heth's division reached Cashtown on the 29th, and the following morning [J. Johnston] Pettigrew's brigade, sent by General Heth to procure supplies at Gettysburg, found it occupied by the enemy. Being ignorant of the extent of his force, General Pettigrew was unwilling to hazard an attack with his single brigade and returned to Cashtown.

General Hill arrived with [William] Pender's division in the evening, and the following morning [July 1st] advanced with these two divisions, accompanied by [William J.] Pegram's and [David G.] McIntosh's battalions of artillery, to ascertain the strength of the enemy, whose force was supposed to consist chiefly of cavalry. The leading division under General Heth found the enemy's videttes [sentries] about three miles west of Gettysburg, and continued to advance until within a mile of the town, when two brigades were sent forward to reconnoitre. They drove in the advance of the enemy very gallantly, but subsequently encountered largely-superior numbers, and were compelled to retire with loss, Brigadier-general [James] Archer, commanding one of the brigades, being taken prisoner. General Heth then prepared for action, and as soon as Pender arrived to support him was ordered by General Hill to advance. The artillery was placed in position and the engagement opened with vigor. General Heth pressed the enemy steadily back, breaking his first and second lines, and attacking his third with great resolution. About 2:30 p.m. the advance of Ewell's corps, consisting of [Robert E.] Rodes's division, with [Thomas H.] Carter's battalion of artillery, arrived by the Middletown road, and, forming on Heth's left nearly at right angles with his line, became warmly engaged with fresh numbers of the enemy. Heth's troops, having suffered heavily in their protracted contest with a superior force, were relieved by Pender's, and Early, coming up by the Heidlersburg road soon afterward, took position on the left of Rodes, when a general advance was made.

The enemy gave way on all sides and was driven through Gettysburg with great loss. Major-general [J. F.] Reynolds, who was in command, was killed. More than 5,000 prisoners, exclusive of a large number of wounded, 3 pieces of artillery, and several colors were captured. Among the prisoners were two brigadier-generals, one of whom was badly wounded. Our own loss was heavy, including a number of officers, among whom were Major-general Heth slightly, and Brigadier-general [A. M.] Scales of Pender's division severely, wounded. The enemy retired to a range of hills south of Gettysburg, where he displayed a strong force of infantry and artillery.

It was ascertained from the prisoners that we had been engaged with two corps of the army formerly commandered by General Hooker, and that the remainder of that army, under General [George G.] Meade, was approaching Gettysburg. Without information as to its proximity, the strong position which the enemy had assumed could not be attacked without danger of exposing the four divisions present, already weakened and exhausted by a long and bloody struggle, to overwhelming numbers of fresh troops. General Ewell was therefore instructed to carry the hill [Culp's Hill] occupied by the enemy if he found it practicable, but to avoid a general engagement until the arrival of the other divisions of the army, which were ordered to hasten forward. He decided to await [Edward] Johnson's division, which had marched from Carlisle by the road west of the mountains to guard the trains of his corps, and consequently did not reach Gettysburg until a late hour.

In the mean time the enemy occupied the point which General Ewell designed to seize, but in what force could not be ascertained, owing to the darkness. An intercepted dispatch showed that another corps had halted that afternoon four miles from Gettysburg. Under these circumstances it was decided not to attack until the arrival of Longstreet, two of whose divisions … encamped about four miles in rear during the night. [Richard H.] Anderson's division of Hill's corps came up after the engagement.

It had not been intended to deliver a general battle so far from our base unless attacked, but, coming unexpectedly upon the whole Federal army, to withdraw through the mountains with our extensive trains would have been difficult and dangerous. At the same time we were unable to await an attack, as the country was unfavorable for collecting supplies in the presence of the enemy, who could restrain our foraging-parties by holding the mountain passes with local and other troops. A battle had therefore become, in a measure, unavoidable, and the success already gained gave hope of a favorable issue.

## Source

Lee, Robert E. "Report of General R. E. Lee of the Gettysburg Campaign, June to August, 1863." In *Memoirs of Robert E. Lee.* Edited by A. E. Long. New York: J. M. Stoddart and Co., 1886, pp. 594-95.

# Impressions of the Battle from a British Observer

*Sir Arthur James Lyon Fremantle was a British military officer who accompanied the Confederate Army of Northern Virginia as an unofficial observer during the summer of 1863. Fremantle published an account of his experiences, called* Three Months in the Southern States, *one year later, after returning to England. Fremantle's memoir included a treasure trove of information for historians about the attitudes and strategic decisions of General Robert E. Lee's Army of Northern Virginia before, during, and after the Battle of Gettysburg. In the following excerpt, Fremantle describes a supremely confident Confederate force at the close of the first day at Gettysburg.*

*1st July*, Wednesday.—We did not leave our camp till noon, as nearly all General [A. P.] Hill's corps had to pass our quarters on its march towards Gettysburg. One division of [Richard S.] Ewell's also had to join in a little beyond Greenwood, and [James] Longstreet's corps had to bring up the rear.

Soon after starting we got into a pass in the South Mountain, a continuation, I believe, of the Blue Ridge range, which is broken by the Potomac at Harper's Ferry. The scenery through the pass is very fine. The first troops, alongside of whom we rode, belonged to Johnson's division of Ewell's corps. Among them I saw, for the first time, the celebrated "Stonewall" Brigade, formerly commanded by Jackson. In appearance the men differ little from other Confederate soldiers, except, perhaps, that the brigade contains more elderly men and fewer boys. All (except, I think, one regiment) are Virginians. As they have nearly always been on detached duty, few of them knew General Longstreet, except by reputation. Numbers of them asked me whether the General in front was Longstreet; and when I answered in the affirmative, many would run on a hundred yards in order to take a good look at him. This I take to be an immense compliment from any soldier on a long march.

At 2 P. M. firing became distinctly audible in our front, but although it increased as we progressed, it did not seem to be very heavy....

At 3 P. M. we began to meet wounded men coming to the rear, and the number of these soon increased most rapidly, some hobbling alone, others on stretchers carried by the ambulance corps, and others in the ambulance wagons. Many of the latter were stripped nearly naked, and displayed very bad wounds. This spectacle, so revolting to a person unaccustomed to such sights, produced no impression whatever upon the advancing troops, who certainly go under fire with the most perfect nonchalance. They show no enthusiasm or

173

excitement, but the most complete indifference. This is the effect of two years' almost uninterrupted fighting.

We now began to meet Yankee prisoners coming to the rear in considerable numbers. Many of them were wounded, but they seemed already to be on excellent terms with their captors, with whom they had commenced swapping canteens, tobacco, &c. Among them was a Pennsylvanian Colonel, a miserable object from a wound in his face. In answer to a question, I heard one of them remark, with a laugh, "We're pretty nigh whipped already." We next came to a Confederate soldier carrying a Yankee color, belonging, I think, to a Pennsylvania regiment, which he told me he had just captured.

At 4.30 P. M. we came in sight of Gettysburg, and joined General [Robert E.] Lee and General Hill, who were on the top of one of the ridges which form the peculiar feature of the country around Gettysburg. We could see the enemy retreating up one of the opposite ridges, pursued by the Confederates with loud yells. The position into which the enemy had been driven was evidently a strong one. His right appeared to rest on a cemetery, on the top of a high ridge to the right of Gettysburg, as we looked at it.

General Hill now came up and told me he had been very unwell all day, and in fact he looks very delicate. He said he had had two of his divisions engaged, and had driven the enemy four miles into his present position, capturing a great many prisoners, some cannon, and some colors. He said, however, that the Yankees had fought with a determination unusual to them. He pointed out a railway cutting, in which they had made a good stand; also, a field in the centre of which he had seen a man plant the regimental color, round which the regiment had fought for some time with much obstinacy, and when at last it was obliged to retreat, the color-bearer retired last of all, turning round every now and then to shake his fist at the advancing rebels. General Hill said he felt quite sorry when he saw this gallant Yankee meet his doom.

General Ewell had come up at 3.30, on the enemy's right (with part of his corps), and completed his discomfiture. General [John] Reynolds, one of the best Yankee generals, was reported killed. Whilst we were talking, a message arrived from General Ewell, requesting Hill to press the enemy in the front, whilst he performed the same operation on his right. The pressure was accordingly applied in a mild degree, but the enemy were too strongly posted, and it was too late in the evening for a regular attack.

The town of Gettysburg was now occupied by Ewell, and was full of Yankee dead and wounded. I climbed up a tree in the most commanding place I could find, and could form a pretty good general idea of the enemy's position, although the tops of the ridges being covered with pine-woods, it was very difficult to see anything of the troops concealed in them. The firing ceased about dark, at which time I rode back with General Longstreet and his Staff to his headquarters at Cashtown, a little village eight miles from Gettysburg. At that time troops were pouring along the road, and were being marched towards the position they are to occupy tomorrow.

In the fight to-day nearly 6,000 prisoners had been taken, and 10 guns. About 20,000 men must have been on the field on the Confederate side. The enemy had two *corps d'armée* [army corps] engaged. All the prisoners belong, I think, to the 1st and 11th corps. This day's work is called a "brisk little scurry," and all anticipate a "big battle" to-morrow.

I observed that the artillery-men in charge of the horses dig themselves little holes like graves, throwing up the earth at the upper end. They ensconce themselves in these holes when under fire.

At supper this evening, General Longstreet spoke of the enemy's position as being "very formidable." He also said that they would doubtless intrench themselves strongly during the night....

The Staff officers spoke of the battle as a certainty, and the universal feeling in the army was one of profound contempt for an enemy whom they have beaten so constantly, and under so many disadvantages.

## Source

Fremantle, A. J. L. *Three Months in the Southern States: April, June 1863.* Mobile, AL: S. H. Goetzel, 1864, pp. 127-29. Retrieved from http://docsouth.unc.edu/imls/fremantle/fremantle.html. Reprinted in *Two Witnesses at Gettysburg,* edited by Gary W. Gallagher, Wiley-Blackwell, 2009, 106-10.

## Longstreet and Lee Debate Strategy before the Second Day of Battle

*At the close of the first day of battle at Gettysburg, General Robert E. Lee, commander of the Confederate Army of Northern Virginia, supervised the placement of troops for the evening and gathered information about the enemy's position in order to craft a battlefield strategy for the next day. During these preparations it became clear that Lee and his closest advisor, General James Longstreet, had very different ideas about how the Army of Northern Virginia should proceed. The following passage from Longstreet's memoirs showcases the author's doubts about Lee's course of action—as well as his efforts to show loyalty to his commander.*

[General Robert E. Lee] ... rode on to Seminary Ridge in time to view the closing operations of the engagement. The Union troops were in disorder, climbing Cemetery Heights, the Confederates following through the streets of Gettysburg. Two other divisions of Confederates were up soon after, E. Johnson's of the Second and R. H. Anderson's of the Third Corps.

After a long wait I left orders for the troops to follow the trains of the Second Corps, and rode to find General Lee. His head-quarters were on Seminary Ridge at the crossing of the Cashtown road.... Dismounting and passing the usual salutation, I drew my glasses and made a studied view of the position upon which the enemy was rallying his forces, and of the lay of the land surrounding. General Lee was engaged at the moment. He had announced beforehand that he would not make aggressive battle in the enemy's country. After the survey and in consideration of his plans,—noting movements of detachments of the enemy on the Emmitsburg road, the relative positions for maneuver, the lofty perch of the enemy, the rocky slopes from it, all marking the position clearly defensive,—I said "We could not call the enemy to position better suited to our plans. All that we have to do is to file around his left and secure good ground between him and his capital." This, when said, was thought to be the opinion of my commander as much as my own. I was not a little surprised, therefore, at his impatience, as, striking the air with his closed hand, he said, "If he is there to-morrow I will attack him."...

I was at a loss to understand his nervous condition, and supported the suggestion so far as to say, "If he is there to-morrow it will be because he wants you to attack."...

*[When Lee stands by his orders the next morning, Longstreet dutifully carries them out, even after one of his officers expresses misgivings.]*

176

General [John Bell] Hood was ordered to send his select scouts in advance, to go through the woodlands and act as vedettes [sentries], in the absence of cavalry, and give information of the enemy, if there. The double line marched up the slope and deployed—[Lafayette] McLaws on the right of Anderson, Hood's division on his right, McLaws near the crest of the plateau in front of the Peach Orchard, Hood spreading and enveloping [Union general Daniel] Sickles's left. The former was readily adjusted to ground from which to advance or defend. Hood's front was very rugged, with no field for artillery, and very rough for advance of infantry. As soon as he passed the Emmitsburg road, he sent to report of the great advantage of moving on by his right around to the enemy's rear. His scouting parties had reported that there was nothing between them and the enemy's trains. He was told that the move to the right had been proposed the day before and rejected; that General Lee's orders were to guide my left by the Emmitsburg road....

General Hood appealed again and again for the move to the right, but, to give more confidence to his attack, he was reminded that the move to the right had been carefully considered by our chief and rejected in favor of his present orders.

## Source

Longstreet, James. *From Manassas to Appomattox: Memoirs of the Civil War in America*. Philadelphia: J. B. Lippincott, 1896, pp. 357-58, 367-68.

# Chamberlain Describes the Battle of Little Round Top

*The Battle of Little Round Top was one of the pivotal clashes of the second day at the Battle of Gettysburg. Confederate forces led by General John Bell Hood nearly seized control of the hill from outnumbered Union defenders. If the offensive had succeeded, the Rebels would have been able to launch devastating artillery and infantry attacks on Union lines directly to the north. But the Union troops finally broke the offensive with a desperate bayonet attack ordered by Colonel Joshua Lawrence Chamberlain, regimental commander of the 20th Maine. The following description of this famous clash is taken from a firsthand account of the battle written by Chamberlain himself.*

## DOUBLE-QUICK TO THE HAVOC OF BATTLE

… The fight was desperate already. We passed along its rear, first getting a glimpse of the Peach Orchard on the right, where our troops were caught between [Henry] Heth's Corps on Seminary Ridge and [James] Longstreet's Corps fast arriving on the Emmitsburg Road—and the havoc was terrible. We passed on to the Wheat-field where heroic men standing bright as golden grain were ravaged by Death's wild reapers from the woods. Here we halted to be shown our places. We had a momentary glimpse of the Third Corps left in front of Round Top, and the fearful struggle at the Devil's Den, and [John B.] Hood's out-flanking troops swarming beyond. Our halt was brief, but our senses alert. I saw our First and Second Brigades go on to the roaring woods, between the Peach Orchard and the Wheat-field.

## THE RACE TO LITTLE ROUND TOP

In another instant, a staff officer from [Maj.] General [G. K.] Warren rushed up to find [Maj. Gen. George] Sykes, our Corps Commander, to beg him to send a brigade at least, to seize Little Round Top before the enemy's surging waves should overwhelm it. Other supplications were in the air; calling for aid everywhere. Our [Strong] Vincent, soldierly and self-reliant, hearing this entreaty for Round Top, waited word from no superior, but taking the responsibility ordered us to turn and push for Round Top at all possible speed, and dashed ahead to study how best to place us. We broke to the right and rear, found a rude log bridge over Plum Run, and a rough farm-road leading to the base of the mountain. Here, as we could, we took the double-quick.…

## HOLD THE LINE AT ALL COSTS

As we neared the summit of the mountain, the shot so raked the crest that we had to keep our men below it to save their heads, although this did not wholly avert the visits of tree-tops and splinters of rock and iron, while the boulders and clefts and pitfalls in our path made it seem like the replica of the evil "den" across the sweetly named Plum Run.

Reaching the southern face of Little Round Top, I found Vincent there, with intense poise and look. He said with a voice of awe, as if translating the tables of the eternal law, "I place you here! This is the left of the Union line. You understand. You are to hold this ground at all costs!" I did understand—full well; but had more to learn about costs....

## A LULL, THEN THE CRASH OF HELL

Ten minutes had not passed. Suddenly the thunder of artillery and crash of iron that had all the while been roaring over the Round Top crests stopped short.

We understood this, too. The storming lines, that had swept past the Third Corps' flank, had got up the base of Little Round Top, and under the range and reach of their guns. They were close upon us among the rocks, we knew, unseen, because so near. In a minute more came the roll of musketry. It struck the exposed right center of our brigade.

Promptly answered, repulsed, and renewed again and again, it soon reached us, still extending. Two brigades of Hood's Division had attacked—Texas and Alabama. The Fourth Alabama reached our right, the Forty-seventh Alabama joined and crowded in, but gradually, owing to their echelon advance. Soon seven companies of this regiment were in our front. We had all we could stand. My attention was sharply called, now here, now there. In the thick of the fight and smoke, Lieutenant [James H.] Nichols, a bright officer near our center, ran up to tell me something queer was going on in his front, behind those engaging us.

## THE GRAY IS FLANKING US!

I sprang forward, mounted a great rock in the midst of his company line, and was soon able to resolve the "queer" impression into positive knowledge. Thick groups in gray were pushing up along the smooth dale between the Round Tops in a direction to gain our left flank. There was no mistaking this. If they could hold our attention by a hot fight in front while they got in force on that flank, it would be bad for us and our whole defence. How many were coming we could not know. We were rather too busy to send out a reconnaissance. If a strong force should gain our rear, our brigade would be caught as by a mighty shears-blade, and be cut and crushed. What would follow it was easy to foresee. This must not be. Our orders to hold that ground had to be liberally interpreted. That front had to be held, and that rear covered. Something must be done,— quickly and coolly. I called the captains and told them my tactics: To keep the front at the hottest without special regard to its need or immediate effect, and at the same time, as they found opportunity, to take side steps to the left, coming gradually into one rank, file-closers and all. Then I took the colors with their guard and placed them at our extreme left, where a great boulder gave token and support; thence bending back at a right angle the whole body gained ground leftward and made twice our original front. And were not so long doing it. This was a difficult movement to execute under such a fire, requiring coolness as well as heat. Of rare quality were my officers and men. I shall never cease to admire and honor them for what they did in this desperate crisis.

*[Confederate forces made a deep push on the Union's left flank at Little Round Top. The Federal force only barely repulsed these attacks, thanks in part to the brave leadership of Colonel Strong Vincent of the 83rd Pennsylvania Infantry and Patrick O'Rorke of the 140th New York, both of whom were killed.]*

## TO THE RESCUE OR ALL IS LOST!

… The roar of all this tumult reached us on the left, and heightened the intensity of our resolve. Meanwhile the flanking column worked around to our left and joined with those before us in a fierce assault, which lasted with increasing fury for an intense hour. The two lines met and broke and mingled in the shock. The crush of musketry gave way to cuts and thrusts, grapplings and wrestlings. The edge of conflict swayed to and from, with wild whirlpools and eddies. At times I saw around me more of the enemy than of my own men: gaps opening, swallowing, closing again with sharp convulsive energy; squads of stalwart men who had cut their way through us, disappearing as if translated. All around, strange, mingled roar-shouts of defiance, rally, and desperation; and underneath, murmured entreaty and stifled moans; gasping prayers, snatches of Sabbath song, whispers of loved names; everywhere men torn and broken, staggering, creeping quivering on the earth, and dead faces with strangely fixed eyes staring stark into the sky. Things which cannot be told—nor dreamed.

How men held on, each one knows, not I. But manhood commands admiration. There was one fine young fellow, who had been cut down early in the fight with a ghastly wound across his forehead, and who I had thought might possibly be saved with prompt attention. So I had sent him back to our little field hospital, at least to die in peace. Within a half-hour, in a desperate rally I saw that noble youth amidst the rolling smoke as an apparition from the dead, with bloody bandage for the only covering of his head, in the thick of the fight, high-borne and pressing on as they that shall see death no more. I shall know him when I see him again, on whatever shore!

## THE COLORS STAND ALONE…

When that mad carnival lulled,—from some strange instinct in human nature and without any reason in the situation that can be seen—when the battling edges drew asunder, there stood our little line, groups and gaps, notched like saw-teeth, but sharp as steel, tempered in infernal heats like a magic sword of the Goths. We were on the appointed and entrusted line. We had held ground—flat "at all costs!"

But sad surprise! It had seemed to us we were all the while holding our own, and had never left it. But now that the smoke dissolved, we saw our dead and wounded all out in front of us, mingled with more of the enemy. They were scattered all the way down to the very feet of the baffled hostile line now rallying in the low shrubbery for a new onset [offensive]. We could not wait for this. They knew our weakness now. And they were gathering force. No place for tactics now! The appeal must be to primal instincts of human nature! . . .

## THE LAST CARTRIDGE AND BARE STEEL

The silence and the doubt of the momentary lull were quickly dispelled. The formidable Fifteenth Alabama, repulsed and as we hoped dispersed, now in solid and orderly array—still more than twice our numbers—came rolling through the fringe of chaparral on our left. No dash; no yells; no demonstrations for effect; but settled purpose and determination! We opened on them as best we could. The fire was returned, cutting us to the quick. The Forty-Seventh Alabama had rallied on our right. We were enveloped in fire, and sure to be overwhelmed in fact when the great surge struck us. Whatever might be other where, what was here before us was evident; these far outnumbering, confident eyes, yet watching for a sign of weakness. Already I could see the bold flankers on their right darting out and creeping and creeping catlike under the smoke to gain our left, thrown back as it was…. Our thin line was broken, and the enemy were in rear of the whole Round Top defense—infantry, artillery, humanity itself—with the Round Top and the day theirs. Now, too, our fire was slackening; our last rounds of shot had been fired; what I had sent for could not get to us. I saw the faces of my men one after another, when they had fired their last cartridge, turn anxiously towards mine for a moment; then square to the front again. To the front for them lay death; to the rear what they would die to save....

Just then—so will a little incident fleck a brooding cloud of doom with a tint of human tenderness—brave, warm-hearted Lieutenant [Holman S.] Melcher, of the Color Company, whose Captain and nearly half his men were down, came up and asked if he might take his company and go forward and pick up one or two of his men left wounded on the field, and bring them in before the enemy got too near. This would be a most hazardous move in itself and in this desperate moment, we could not break our line. But I admired him. With a glance, he understood, I answered, "Yes, sir, in a moment! I am about to order a charge!"

Not a moment was about to be lost! Five minutes more of such a defensive, and the last roll-call would sound for us! Desperate as the chances were, there was nothing for it, but to take the offensive. I stepped to the colors. The men turned towards me. One word was enough,—"BAYONET!"—It caught like fire, and swept along the ranks. The men took it up with a shout, one could not say, whether from the pit, or the song of the morning star! It was vain to order "Forward." No mortal could have heard it in the mighty hosanna that was winging the sky. Nor would he wait to hear. There are things still as of the first creation, "whose seed is in itself." The grating clash of steel in fixing bayonets told its own story; the color rose in front; the whole line quivered for the start; the edge of the left-wing rippled, swung, tossed among the rocks, straightened, changed curve from scimitar to sickle-shape; and the bristling archers swooped down upon the serried host—down into the face of half a thousand! Two hundred men!

It was a great right wheel. Our left swung first. The advancing foe stopped, tried to make a stand amidst the trees and boulders, but the frenzied bayonets pressing through every space, forced a constant settling to the rear. [Walter] Morrill with his detached company and the remnants of our valorous sharpshooters, who had held the enemy so long in check on the slopes of the Great Round Top, now fell upon the flank of the retiring crowd, and it turned to full retreat, some up amidst the crags of Great Round Top, but most down the smooth vale towards their own main line on Plum Run. This tended to mass them before our center. Here their stand was more stubborn. At the first dash the commanding officer I happened to confront, coming on fiercely, sword in one hand and big navy revolver in the other, fires one barrel almost in my face; but seeing the quick saber-point at his throat, reverses arms, gives sword and pistol into my hands and yields himself prisoner. I took him at his word, but could not give him further attention. I passed him over into the custody of a brave sergeant at my side, to whom I gave the sword as emblem of his authority, but kept the pistol with its loaded barrels, which I thought might come handy soon, as indeed it did.

Ranks were broken; many retired before us somewhat hastily; some threw their muskets to the ground—even loaded; sunk on their knees, threw up their hands, calling out, "We surrender. Don't kill us!" As if we wanted to do that! We kill only to resist killing. And these were manly men, whom we would befriend, and by no means kill, if they came our way in peace and good will. Charging right through and over these, we struck the second line of the Forty-seventh Alabama doing their best to stand, but offering little resistance. Their Lieutenant-Colonel as I passed—and a fine gentleman was Colonel [M. J.] Bulger—introduced himself as my prisoner, and as he was wounded, I had him cared for as best we could. Still swinging to the right as a great gate on its hinges, we swept the front clean of assailants....

## TWO FOR EVERY MAN OF US

When we reached the front of the Forty-fourth New York, I thought it far enough. Beyond on the right the Texas Brigade had rallied or rendezvoused, I took thought of that. Most of the fugitives before us, rather than run the gauntlet of our whole brigade, had taken the shelter of the rocks of Great Round Top, on our left, as we now faced. It was hazardous to be so far out, in the very presence of so many baffled but far from beaten veterans of Hood's renowned division. A sudden rush on either flank might not only cut us off, but cut in behind us and seize that vital point which it was our orders and our trust to hold. But it was no light task to get our men to stop. They were under the momentum of their deed. They thought they were "on the road to Richmond." They had to be reasoned with, persuaded, but at last faced about and marched back to that dedicated crest with swelling hearts.

Not without sad interest and service was the return. For many of the wounded had to be gathered up. There was a burden, too, of the living. Nearly four hundred prisoners remained in our hands—two for every man of ours.

## Source

Chamberlain, Joshua Lawrence. "Through Blood and Fire at Gettysburg." *Hearst's Magazine*, June 1913, pp. 894-909.

## Meade Decides to Stay Put after Day Two at Gettysburg

*After the sun set on the battlefield at Gettysburg on July 2, Union general George G. Meade and his*
*chief officers gathered together to take stock of the situation. Meade later recalled this meeting in his*
*wartime memoirs. In the following excerpt from that volume, written by Meade in the third-person,*
*the general recalls that he and his corps commanders agreed that the wisest course of action would*
*be for their troops to maintain their defensive positions atop the hills and ridges south of Gettsyburg.*

When the action finally ceased, and comparative quiet reigned, General [George] Meade summoned his corps commanders to headquarters, in order to obtain from them information as to the condition of their respective commands, and to confer with them as to what action, if any, should be taken on the following day.

It was after nine o'clock before the corps commanders had assembled in the one little room which had served the original occupants of the house for all purposes of living. Here, in these close quarters, were a bed, a table, and a few chairs and other appurtenances, on which sat or reclined, as convenience dictated as most restful, Generals [John] Sedgwick, [Henry] Slocum, [Winfield Scott] Hancock, [Oliver O.] Howard, [George] Sykes, [John] Newton, [David B.] Birney, A. S. Williams, and [John] Gibbon. As officer after officer arrived, each in turn reported what had taken place on his immediate front during the day, and the extent of his losses so far as they could be obtained. The result of the day's fighting having been thus ascertained, a general conversation ensued, in which the position of the army, the probability of an attempt on the part of General Lee to make a flank movement around its left, and the dispositions which, in that event, should be made, were thoroughly discussed. The conversation had taken a very wide range, and continued for a long time, when General Meade finally summarized the points to be decided and submitted them in the form of a series of questions. These were as to whether or not, under the existing circumstances, it would be more advisable for the army to remain in the position which it then held or to retire to one nearer its base. Again, if it were decided to maintain its position, should the army attack, or should it await the attack of the enemy. And, in the latter event, for how long should the army await the enemy's attack. Commencing with General Gibbon, the youngest in rank, each officer replied in succession. It was the unanimous opinion that the army should maintain the position then held and await further attack before assuming the offensive. This opinion agreed entirely with General Meade's own views as to the proper course to adopt. He did not take a prominent part in the discussion. He had clearly stated what his instructions had been and the conclusion to be drawn from the results of the day's fighting. He had from the first felt that the enemy would again attack. In consequence of this, and while the conference was still progressing, he sent the following dispatch to General [Henry] Halleck, which clearly shows what he had resolved to do:

Headquarters Army of the Potomac, July 2, 1863, 11 p.m.

General Halleck:

The enemy attacked me about 4 p.m. this day, and after one of the severest contests of the war, was repulsed at all points. We have suffered considerably in killed and wounded; among the former are Brigadier General Paul Zook, and among the wounded Generals [Dan] Sickles, [Francis] Barlow, [Charles K.] Graham, and [Gouvernor] Warren slightly. We have taken a large number of prisoners. I shall remain in my present position to-morrow, but am not prepared to say, until better advised of the condition of the army, whether my operations will be of an offensive or defensive character.

George G. Meade,
Major General

The confidence of us all as to the ability of the army to hold its position against any direct attack of the enemy was manifest. There was universal satisfaction when, at the close of the vote in favor of the army's maintaining its position, General Meade said quietly, though decidedly: "Such then is the decision." It was after midnight before the conference broke up and the officers departed for their several head-quarters. As they were leaving, General Meade had a few moments' conversation with General Gibbon. During the course of their remarks reference was made to the majority of the officers present having voted in favor of acting on the defensive and awaiting the action of General Lee  General Meade said: "Gibbon, if Lee attacks me to-morrow it will be on *your front*." Gibbon expressed surprise and asked why he thought so. "Because," replied General Meade, "he has tried my left and failed, and has tried my right and failed; now, if he concludes to try it again, he will try the centre, right on your front." To this Gibbon promptly responded, "Well, general, I hope he does, and if he does, we shall whip him."

## Source

Meade, George G. *The Life and Letters of George Gordon Meade.* Vol. II. New York: Charles Scribner's Sons, 1913, pp. 95-97.

## A Rebel Officer Remembers Pickett's Charge

*On July 3—the third and final day of the Battle of Gettysburg—Confederate general Robert E. Lee ordered a major offensive against entrenched Union forces atop Cemetery Ridge. The assault, which came to be known as Pickett's Charge, was a disaster for the Rebels. Its failure forced Lee and his Army of Northern Virginia to retreat from Gettysburg and return to Virginia. In the following account, a captain of the 18th Virginia infantry named Henry T. Owen provides his recollections of that bloody and unsuccessful charge.*

Long double lines of infantry came pouring out of the woods and bottoms, across ravines and little valleys, hurrying on to the positions assigned them in the column. Two separate lines of double ranks were formed a hundred yards apart, and in the center of the column was placed the division of Pickett, said to be "the flower of Lee's army." ...

The column of attack, composed of [Brig. Gen. Cadmus M.] Wilcox's Brigade, [Major General George] Pickett's and [Maj. Gen. Henry] Heth's Divisions and several other commands, detached for this duty, had been variously estimated, but probably numbered about 13,000 troops, the command of the whole line given to General Pickett, a brave and fearless officer and a fit leader of this forlorn hope, thrown forward to retrieve disaster or turn by fierce conflict the waning fortunes of a dying cause.

Riding out in front, Pickett made a brief, animated address to the troops and closed by saying to his own division, "Charge the enemy and remember old Virginia." Then came the command in a strong, clear voice, "Forward! Guide center! March!" and the column, with a front of more than half a mile, moved grandly up the slope. Meade's guns opened upon the column as it appeared above the crest of the ridge, but it neither paused nor faltered. Round shot, bounding along the plain, tore through their ranks and ricocheted around them; shells exploded incessantly in blinding, dazzling flashes before them, behind them, overhead and among them. Frightful gaps were made from center to flank, yet on swept the column and as it advanced the men steadily closed up the wide rents made along the line in a hundred places at every discharge of the murderous batteries in front.

A long line of skirmishers, prostrate in the tall grass, firing at the column since it came within view, rose up within fifty yards, fired a volley into its front, then trotted on before it, turning and firing back as fast as they could reload. The column moved on at a quick step with shouldered arms, and the fire of the skirmish line was not returned. Half way over the field an order ran down the line, "left oblique," which was promptly obeyed and the direction changed forty-five degrees from the front to the left. Men looking away, far off toward the left flank, saw that the supporting columns there were crumbling and melting rapidly away. General Pickett sent his brother, Maj. Charles Pickett, galloping swiftly to rally, if possible, the wavering lines, saying to him, "Unless they support us on the left my division will be cut to pieces." Major Pickett and other officers rode among the breaking battalions and vainly attempted to restore order, but hundreds and thousands of fugitives from the front could be seen fleeing from the field and went rushing pell-mell toward the rear like dry leaves before a gale. Order was not restored upon the left and Pickett's support there was gone excepting some brave Tennesseans and North Carolinians, who never wavered in the storm, but closing up by the side of Pickett's Virginians went as far, fought as long, bled as freely, and fell as thick as Pickett's men.

The command now came along the line, "Front, forward!" and the column resumed its direction straight down upon the center of the enemy's position. Some men now looking to the right saw that the troops there had entirely disappeared, but how or when they left was not known. The enemy in front, occupying an elevated position and watching closely every movement of the advancing columns, say "the right gave way first, then the left broke up and fled the field, but the massive center, composed of Pickett's veterans of firm nerve, wounded in scores of battles, were coming sternly on." Guns hitherto employed in firing at the troops on the right and left sent a shower of shells after the fleeing fugitives and then trained upon the center, where the storm burst in tenfold fury, as converging batteries sent a concentrated fire of shot and shell in, through and around the heroic column.

The destruction of life in the ranks of that advancing host was fearful beyond precedent, officers going down by dozens and the men by scores and fifties. [Brig. Gen. James L.] Kemper had gone down terribly mangled, but [Brig. Gen. Richard B.] Garnett still towered unhurt and rode up and down the front line, saying in a strong, calm voice, "Faster, men! Faster! Close up and step out faster, but don't double quick!" The column was approaching the Emmitsburg Road, where a line of infantry, stationed behind a stone fence, was pouring in a heavy fire of musketry. A scattering fire was opened along the front of the division upon the line, when Garnett galloped along the line and called out, "Cease firing," and his command was promptly obeyed, showing the wonderful discipline of the men, who reloaded their guns, shouldered arms and kept on without slackening their pace, which was still a "quick step."

The stone fence was carried without a struggle, the infantry and the skirmish line swept away before the division like trash before the broom.... We were now four hundred yards from the foot of Cemetery Hill, when away off to the right, nearly half a mile, there appeared in the open field a line of men at right angles with our own, a long, dark mass, dressed in blue and coming down at a "double-quick" upon the unprotected right flank of Pickett's men, with their muskets "upon the right shoulder shift," their battle flags dancing and fluttering in the breeze created by their own rapid motion and their burnished bayonets glistening above their heads like forest twigs covered with sheets of sparkling ice when shaken by a blast. Garnett galloped along the line saying, "Faster, men! Steady! Don't double quick. Save your wind and your ammunition for the final charge!" and then went down among the dead and his clarion voice was no more heard above the roar of battle.

The enemy were now seen strengthening their lines where the blow was expected to strike by hurrying up reserves from the right and left, the columns from opposite directions passing each other double along our front like the fingers of a man's two hands locking together....

There it was again! And again! A sound filling the air above, below and around us, like the blast through the top of a dry cedar or the whirring sound made by the sudden flight of a flock of quail. It was grape and canister and the column broke forward into a double quick and rushed toward the stone wall where forty cannon were belching forth grape and canister twice and thrice a minute. A hundred yards from the stone wall the flanking party on the right, coming down on a heavy run, halted suddenly within fifty yards and poured a deadly storm of musket balls into Pickett's men, double-quicking across their front, and under this terrible crossfire the men reeled and staggered between falling comrades, and the right came pressing down upon the center, crowding the companies into confusion. But all knew the purpose to carry the heights in front, and the mingled mass, from fifteen to thirty deep, rushed toward the stone wall, while a few hundred men, without orders, faced to the right and fought the flanking party there, although [outnumbered] fifty to one and for a time held them at bay....

The enemy were falling back in front, while officers were seen among their breaking lines striving to maintain their ground. Pickett's men were within a few feet of the stone wall when the artillery delivered their last fire from guns shotted to the muzzle—a blaze fifty feet long went through the charging, surging host with a gaping rent to the rear but the survivors mounted the wall, then over and onward, rushed up the hill after the gunners who waved their rammers in the face of Pickett's men and sent up cheer after cheer as they felt admiration for the gallant charge.

On swept the column over ground covered with dead and dying men, where the earth seemed to be on fire, the smoke dense and suffocating, the sun shot out, flames blazing on every side, friend could hardly be distinguished from foe, but the division, in the shape of an inverted "V" with the point flattened, pushed forward, fighting, falling, and melting away, till halfway up the hill they were met by a powerful body of fresh troops charging down upon them, and this remnant of about a thousand men was hurled back out into the clover field. Brave [Brig. Gen. Lewis A.] Armistead went down among the enemy's guns, mortally wounded, but was last seen leaning upon one elbow, slashing at the gunners to prevent them from firing at his retreating men. Out in front of the breastworks the men showed a disposition to reform for another charge, and an officer looking at the frowning heights, with blood trickling down the side of his face, inquired of another, "What shall we do?" The answer was, "If we get reinforcements soon we can take that hill yet." But no reinforcements came, none were in sight, and about a thousand men fled to the rear over dead and wounded, mangled, groaning, dying men, scattered thick, far and wide, while shot and shell tore up the earth and minie balls flew around them for more than a thousand yards.

## Source

Owen, Henry T. "Pickett at Gettysburg." *Philadelphia Weekly Times,* March 26, 1881. Reprinted in *The New Annals of the Civil War,* edited by Peter Cozzens and Robert I. Girardi. Mechanicsburg, PA: Stackpole, 2004, pp. 300-303.

## A Yankee Soldier Recalls Pickett's Charge

*The final great clash at the Battle of Gettysburg was Pickett's Charge, a ferocious but ultimately unsuccessful attempt by Confederate general Robert E. Lee to overrun the defenses of Union general George G. Meade. The failure of Pickett's Charge left Lee no choice but to withdraw his Army of Northern Virginia back to the South. The following account of Pickett's Charge and its aftermath was written by Franklin Sawyer, lieutenant-colonel of the Eighth Ohio Volunteers, which was part of the Union line that repulsed the Confederate assault.*

In our front all was quiet until between twelve and one o'clock, when a terrific cannonade opened from the rebel guns, about one hundred and fifty in number, forming a semi-circle around our position. This fire was replied to by at least an equal number of our own guns.

Nothing more terrific than this storm of artillery can be imagined. The missiles of both armies passed over our heads. The roar of the guns was deafening, the air was soon clouded with smoke, and the shriek and startling crack of exploding shell above, around, and in our midst; the blowing up of our caissons in our rear; the driving through the air of fence-rails, posts, and limbs of trees; the groans of dying men, the neighing of frantic and wounded horses, created a scene of absolute horror. Our line of skirmishers was kept out to watch any advance; but the rest of the men kept well down in the cut of the road. Here for nearly two hours we sat stock still, and not a word was uttered. Only two of the men were killed during the cannonade, and they were literally cut in two. Capt. [J. E.] Gregg, who was then serving on Col. [Samuel S.] Carroll's Staff as Inspector, had come down just before the fire opened to see how we were getting along, and not being able to return, sat down on a rail with the writer, facing towards the enemy. Presently, a solid shot tore through a pile of rails in our front, passed under our seat between us, and bounded away to our rear. The ricochet of round shot in our vicinity was quite frequent as well as the fragments of shells that exploded in the air.

Finally the artillery ceased firing, and all knew that an assault was the next movement. Soon we saw the long line of rebel infantry emerge from the woods along the rebel front, that had hitherto concealed them.

These troops were the division of Picket [Major General George Pickett], followed by that of [Brigadier General J. Johnston] Pettigrew. They moved up splendidly, deploying into column as they crossed the long, sloping interval between the Second Corps and their base. At first it looked as if their line of march would sweep our position, but as they advanced their direction lay considerably to our left; but soon a strong line, with flags, directed its march immediately upon us.

I formed the few remaining braves in a single line, and as the rebels came within short range of our skirmish line, charged them. Some fell, some run back, most of them, however, threw down their arms and were made prisoners. In this maneuver among the killed was Lieut. Hayden, Co. H. We changed our front, and, taking position by a fence, facing the left flank of the advancing column of rebels, the men were ordered to fire into their flank at will. Hardly a musket had been fired at this time. The front of the column was nearly up the slope, and within a few yards of the line of the Second Corps' front and its batteries, when suddenly a terrific fire from every available gun from the Cemetery to Round Top Mountain burst upon them. The distinct, graceful lines of the rebels underwent an instantaneous transformation.

They were at once enveloped in a dense cloud of smoke and dust. Arms, heads, blankets, guns and knapsacks were thrown and tossed into the clear air. Their track, as they advanced, was strewn with dead and wounded. A moan went up from the field, distinctly to be heard amid the storm of battle; but on they went, too much enveloped in smoke and dust now to permit us to distinguish their lines or movements, for the mass appeared more like a cloud of moving smoke and dust than a column of troops. Still it advanced amid the now deafening roar of artillery and storm of battle.

Suddenly the column gave way, the sloping landscape appeared covered, all at once, with the scattered and retreating foe. A withering sheet of missiles swept after them, and they were torn and tossed and prostrated as they ran. It seemed as if not one would escape. Of the mounted officers who rode so grandly in the advance, not one was to be seen on the field; all had gone down. The Eighth [Ohio] advanced and cut off three regiments, or remnants of regiments, as they passed us, taking their colors, and capturing many prisoners. The colors captured were those of the Thirty-Fourth North Carolina, Thirty-Eighth Virginia, and one that was taken from the captor, Sergt. Miller, Co. G. by a staff officer, the number of the regiment not being remembered.

The battle was now over. The field was covered with the slain and wounded, and everywhere were to be seen white handkerchiefs held up asking for quarter. The rebel loss had been terrible, the victory to the Union army complete.

The Eighth when we received the order to take this position numbered, present for duty, 209 officers and men, of these 102 were killed and wounded....

On the morning of the 4th of July, we collected and buried our dead near a walnut tree in the vicinity of a farm house, marked their graves, and built a rail fence around them.

During the day, the writer, with other officers, visited most of the noted localities of the field. Everywhere were the evidences of a fierce struggle. Dismounted guns, exploded caissons and limbers, hundreds of dead horses, piles of broken and bent muskets, splintered trees, broken tomb stones at Cemetery Hill, demolished walls, riddled houses and barns met the eye. The ground was plowed and cross-plowed by cannon balls, which had swept through our lines in every direction.

No duties were required of us during the 4th of July, and the men for the greater part of the day remained quietly in their shelter tents, and sought the rest so much needed after the hardships and excitement of the last few days. The rebel army made no further demonstrations of a warlike character during the day.

## Source

Sawyer, Franklin. *A Military History of the 8th Regiment Ohio Vol. Inf'y [Volunteer Infantry]: Its Battles, Marches, and Army Movements.* Cleveland, OH: Fairbanks, 1881, pp. 130-34.

# A Northern Newspaper Hails the Victory at Gettysburg

*The Union triumph at the Battle of Gettysburg sparked a massive wave of joyful newspaper stories and editorials in the cities of the North. The following article, titled "The Unheralded Heroes of Battle," was published in the July 7, 1863, edition of the* New York Times. *The article shows how the clash at Gettysburg gave Northerners a desperately needed infusion of optimism about their ability to win the war.*

The Army of the Potomac has not only won a great battle, and delivered the nation from the gravest peril of the war, but it has triumphantly vindicated its claim to be classed with the veteran and heroic armies that history delights to honor. In all the details that reach us of the Titanic conflict that raged during three days about Gettysburgh, no fact shines out more conspicuously and cheeringly than the fortitude and unflinching valor of our men. They were equal to every crisis in the varying fortunes of the fight. Was it needed to stand firm and unswerving in line of battle, while the air was darkened by the missiles of a hundred guns parked by the rebels to clear the way for an infantry assault?—there was not a corps in the Union Army that was not equal to the duty; and at least half of the corps composing the army at some time during the battle, were called on to endure this fearful, fiery trial. Was it needed after standing for hours before this withering blast of concentrated artillery fire, to receive the shock of the rebel army, massed and thrown forward in columns, in those impetuous charges that have so often before proved successful?—the veteran soldiers of MEADE's army were ready for the fierce onsets, and met them, steel to steel, as only the brave can meet a foe. Was it needed to fall back before overwhelming odds, yet not to fly; but to give blow for blow in falling back, and watch for the opportune moment to change retreat into victory and win back the lost ground? This, too, the Army of the Potomac was capable of, as it again and again illustrated in the three days' battles around Gettysburgh. The annals of warfare are searched in vain for instances of more universal and better sustained valor than characterized our army during the recent combat.

In all the accounts that have reached the public from a score of different observers who watched the battle from different standpoints, there is entire harmony in this particular. In no single instance is there a mention of alarm or flight on the part of any, the most insignificant, column of Union soldiers. Twice or thrice, during the three days' conflict, when the enemy massed his whole

193

army against particular parts of our line to break it, our men were borne back by the mere weight of numbers. It was mechanical pressure, nothing else, the veterans of the Potomac gave way to. But they retired slowly, and in order, with their faces to the foe, lessening his dense ranks at every step by terrible musketry fire, and still more fearful dashes of iron hail from deluging artillery, until the pressure of numbers fairly ceased, and changed to their own side, and then with resurgent shout they turned back the tide of battle, and in turn drove the enemy far beyond the line of his advance. Wounded and slain, and prisoners by thousands, were the trophies that remained in their hands after each fierce onset of the enemy.

Fortune has dealt hardly by the Army of the Potomac. It has been led to battle oft; to victory but seldom. It has borne a part in many of the most sanguinary struggles that have marked modern war. And there has been a singular and painful gradation in the steps by which it reached disasters. This first battle of Bull Run was more than doubled in its casualties by the more honorable but indecisive battle of Fair Oaks. The second bloody struggle was wholly eclipsed by the terrors and carriage of the Seven Days' retreat from before Richmond. The retreat from Richmond was exceeded in disheartening influence upon the country by the retreat upon Washington after POPE's defeat in the second and most bloody battles of Manassas Plains. The battle of Antietam was only an arrest of the succession of reverses. It gave ground of confidence and hope as to what the Army of the Potomac could do. But the reign of hope was brief. For soon came the unredeemed slaughter of Fredericksburgh; and still later, the unaccountable catastrophe of Chancellorsville. This last was the climax of disaster.

After such a history of misfortune, disappointments and defeats, is it not amazing that any soul or spirit was left in the hearts of the men of the Army of the Potomac? What other army of which we have record, has ever lived through such shocking misguidance, such weakening of its country's confidence and such loss of the world's praise, and yet come out of it all with escutcheon clear, with courage unquestioned, with patriotism exalted, and crowned with all the honors and rewards of victory? But the Army of the Potomac has done this thing. It has leaped at once from the depths of its disappointment and gloom to the height of glory and success.

When we remember the past, we must admit that of a truth the patient and long-suffering, the faithful but unappreciated heroes of the Army of the Potomac have wrested their laurels from the hands of reluctant Fortune. They have, in one last great effort, vindicated their own manhood, won the undying gratitude of their country, and extorted the admiration of the world. Leaders may do much for an army, but they can do nothing without courage and tenacity in soldiers. These qualities in the humble rank and file make heroes, found empires, establish great principles, and mould the destiny of nations and races. And so far-reaching, we believe, will be the deeds wrought by our glorious soldiers at Gettysburgh.

There are tens of thousands of bereaved homes in the North … whose woes are connected for the rest of this mortal life with the battles and marches of the Army of the Potomac. But immedicable grief has its halo at last in the honorable fame that is laid up for all who can lay any claim to the glory its heroes have won. History will tell that the battle of Gettysburgh did not win a victory only, but inspired a nation with confidence in its citizen soldiers, and gave to the world a knowledge of martial prowess, worth a hundred battles and victories, in securing from attack the great principles that underlie the fabric of American Free Government.

## Source

"The Unheralded Heroes of Battle." *New York Times,* July 7, 1863. Retrieved from http://www
.nytimes.com/1863/07/07/news/the-unheralded-heroes-of-battle.html?pagewanted=all.

## General Lee Writes Home after Gettysburg

*When General Robert E. Lee and the battered Army of Northern Virginia withdrew from Gettysburg and began the long trek back to Virginia, they were temporarily halted by flooding on the Potomac River. Lee recognized that his army, trapped as it was along the banks of the river, was extremely vulnerable to an attack from the Union's Army of the Potomac. Lee discussed these fears in a letter to his wife, written on July 12, 1863, near Hagerstown, Maryland.*

The consequences of war are horrid enough at best, surrounded by all the ameliorations of civilization and Christianity. I am very sorry for the injuries done the family at Hickory Hill, and particularly that our dear old Uncle Williams, in his eightieth year, should be subjected to such treatment. But we cannot help it, and must endure it. You will, however, learn before this reaches you that our success at Gettysburg was not so great as reported—in fact, that we failed to drive the enemy from his position, and that our army withdrew to the Potomac. Had the river not unexpectedly risen, all would have been well with us; but God, in His all-wise providence, willed otherwise, and our communications have been interrupted and almost cut off. The waters have subsided to about four feet, and, if they continue, by tomorrow, I hope, our communications will be open. I trust that a merciful God, our only hope and refuge, will not desert us in this hour of need, and will deliver us by His almighty hand, that the whole world may recognise His power and all hearts be lifted up in adoration and praise of His unbounded loving-kindness. We must, however, submit to His almighty will, whatever that may be. May God guide and protect us all is my constant prayer.

### Source

Lee, Robert Edward. *Recollections and Letters of General Robert E. Lee.* New York: Doubleday, 1904, pp. 101-2.

# Lincoln's Unsent Letter to Meade

*On July 14, 1863, President Abraham Lincoln learned that Union general George G. Meade and his Army of the Potomac, fresh off their victory at Gettysburg, had passed up a chance to shatter the Confederate Army of Northern Virginia once and for all. After withdrawing from Gettysburg, the enemy had been trapped by floodwaters for several days on the northern side of the Potomac River. Meade, however, decided against launching a full-scale offensive against the weakened Confederates, and on the 14th the Army of Northern Virginia was finally able to cross the Potomac and return to Virginia.*

*Lincoln was extremely upset by this news. When Meade learned of the president's disappointment, he offered to resign. Lincoln did not want Meade's resignation, but he did want to convey his frustration to the general. He subsequently wrote a blunt letter to Meade, which is reprinted below. Ultimately, however, Lincoln decided that the note's scolding tone would do no good, and so he never sent it.*

Major General [George G.] Meade

I have just seen your despatch to Gen. [Henry] Halleck, asking to be relieved of your command, because of a supposed censure of mine. I am very—very—very grateful to you for the magnificent success you gave the cause of the country at Gettysburg; and I am sorry now to be the author of the slightest pain to you. But I was in such deep distress myself that I could not restrain some expression of it. I had been oppressed nearly ever since the battles at Gettysburg, by what appeared to be evidences that yourself, and Gen. [Darius] Couch, and Gen. [William] Smith, were not seeking a collision with the enemy, but were trying to get him across the river without another battle. What these evidences were, if you please, I hope to tell you at some time, when we shall both feel better. The case, summarily stated is this. You fought and beat the enemy at Gettysburg; and, of course, to say the least, his loss was as great as yours. He retreated; and you did not, as it seemed to me, pressingly pursue him; but a flood in the river detained him, till, by slow degrees, you were again upon him. You had at least twenty thousand veteran troops directly with you, and as many more raw ones within supporting distance, all in addition to those who fought with you at Gettysburg; while it was not possible that he had received a single recruit; and yet you stood and let the flood run down, bridges be built, and the enemy move away at his leisure, without attacking him. And Couch and Smith! The latter left Carlisle in time, upon all ordinary calculation, to have aided you in the last battle at Gettysburg; but he did not arrive. At the end of more than ten days, I believe twelve, under constant urging, he reached Hagerstown from Carlisle, which is not an inch over fifty-five miles, if so much. And Couch's movement was very little different.

Again, my dear general, I do not believe you appreciate the magnitude of the misfortune involved in Lee's escape. He was within your easy grasp, and to have closed upon him would, in connection with our other late successes, have ended the war. As it is, the war will be prolonged indefinitely. If you could not safely attack Lee last Monday, how can you possibly do so South of the river, when you can take with you very few more than two thirds of the force you then had in hand? It would be unreasonable to expect, and I do not expect you can now effect much. Your golden opportunity is gone, and I am distressed immeasurably because of it.

I beg you will not consider this a prosecution, or persecution of yourself. As you had learned that I was dissatisfied, I have thought it best to kindly tell you why.

*Abraham Lincoln*

## Source

Lincoln, Abraham. Unsent letter to Major General Meade, July 14, 1863. *Abraham Lincoln: Complete Works, Comprising His Speeches, Letters, State Papers, and Miscellaneous Writings.* Edited by John G. Nicolay and John Hay. Vol. 2. New York: Century Col, 1894, pp. 368-69.

# Lincoln's Gettysburg Address

*On November 19, 1863, President Abraham Lincoln gave one of the most famous speeches in American history. It took him only a few minutes to deliver his remarks at the dedication of the Soldiers' National Cemetery at Gettysburg, Pennsylvania. In the years to come, however, Lincoln's Gettysburg Address would come to be seen as an eloquent and enduring summation of the war's importance in defending American principles of liberty and democracy.*

Four score and seven years ago our fathers brought forth on this continent, a new nation, conceived in Liberty, and dedicated to the proposition that all men are created equal.

Now we are engaged in a great civil war, testing whether that nation, or any nation so conceived and so dedicated, can long endure. We are met on a great battle-field of that war. We have come to dedicate a portion of that field, as a final resting place for those who here gave their lives that that nation might live. It is altogether fitting and proper that we should do this.

But, in a larger sense, we cannot dedicate—we cannot consecrate—we cannot hallow—this ground. The brave men, living and dead, who struggled here, have consecrated it, far above our poor power to add or detract. The world will little note, nor long remember what we say here, but it can never forget what they did here. It is for us the living, rather, to be dedicated here to the unfinished work which they who fought here have thus far so nobly advanced. It is rather for us to be here dedicated to the great task remaining before us—that from these honored dead we take increased devotion to that cause for which they gave the last full measure of devotion—that we here highly resolve that these dead shall not have died in vain—that this nation, under God, shall have a new birth of freedom—and that government of the people, by the people, for the people, shall not perish from the earth.

## Source

Lincoln, Abraham. Gettysburg Address, November 19, 1863. Retrieved from http://americanhistory.si.edu/documentsgallery/exhibitions/gettysburg_address_2.html OR http://www.gettysburgfoundation.org/41.

## Woodrow Wilson Addresses Civil War Veterans at Gettysburg

*In July 1913 veterans of the Battle of Gettysburg from both the Union and Confederate ranks gathered together at the battlefield site for a multi-day commemoration of the famous clash. The event was widely seen as an important symbol of national reconciliation, and it drew many distinguished speakers. One of the speakers was President Woodrow Wilson, whose address to the veterans is reprinted here.*

Friends and Fellow Citizens:

I need not tell you what the Battle of Gettysburg meant. These gallant men in blue and gray sit all about us here. Many of them met upon this ground in grim and deadly struggle. Upon these famous fields and hillsides their comrades died about them. In their presence it were an impertinence to discourse upon how the battle went, how it ended, what it signified! But fifty years have gone by since then, and I crave the privilege of speaking to you for a few minutes of what those fifty years have meant.

What have they meant? They have meant peace and union and vigor, and the maturity and might of a great nation. How wholesome and healing the peace has been! We have found one another again as brothers and comrades in arms, enemies no longer, generous friends rather, our battles long past, the quarrel forgotten—except that we shall not forget the splendid valor, the manly devotion of the men then arrayed against one another, now grasping hands and smiling into each other's eyes. How complete the union has become and how dear to all of us, how unquestioned, how benign and majestic, as State after State has been added to this our great family of free men! How handsome the vigor, the maturity, the might of the great Nation we love with undivided hearts; how full of large and confident promise that a life will be wrought out that will crown its strength with gracious justice and with a happy welfare that will touch all alike with deep contentment! We are debtors to those fifty crowded years; they have made us heirs to a mighty heritage.

But do we deem the Nation complete and finished? These venerable men crowding here to this famous field have set us a great example of devotion and utter sacrifice. They were willing to die that the people might live. But their task is done. Their day is turned into evening. They look to us to perfect what they established. Their work is handed on to us, to be done in another way, but not in another spirit. Our day is not over; it is upon us in full tide.

ment the minority have the right to break up the government whenever they choose. If we fail it will go far to prove the incapability of the people to govern themselves."

It was here at Gettysburg, of course, that Lincoln made the most eloquent and effective statement of this idea. In two minutes—considerably less than I have spoken already—he not only managed to bring together the past, present, and future, but also to weave in two other sets of three images each: continent, nation, battlefield; and birth, death, rebirth. The Gettysburg Address is so familiar to us—many of you virtually know it by heart, like the Lord's Prayer, that we sometimes say or hear it without really thinking about the meaning. When you hear our modern-day Mr. Lincoln deliver those familiar words again today, think about their meaning with respect to these three sets of three images, each interwoven to make an unforgettable pattern:

Four score and seven years in the past, said Lincoln, our fathers gave birth on this continent to a nation conceived in liberty. Today, our generation, said Lincoln, faces a great test whether that nation, or any nation so conceived, can survive. In dedicating the cemetery on this battlefield, the living must take inspiration from those who gave the last full measure of devotion in order to finish the task they so nobly advanced.

Life and death in this passage have a paradoxical but metaphorical relationship: men died that the nation might live, yet metaphorically the old Union also died, and with it would die the institution of slavery. After these deaths, the nation must have a new birth of freedom so that government of, by, and for the people that our fathers brought forth in the past shall live into the vast future, even unto the next millennium.

Will the legacy of one nation, indivisible, that Lincoln left us still be around in another 137 years? No one can say. Perhaps the best words to express what that legacy means today were those written by a 17-year-old girl from Texas a few years ago, in an essay contest connected to a Lincoln exhibit at the Huntington Library and the Chicago Historical Society. This girl's forbearers had immigrated to the United States from India in the 1960s. She wrote that "if the United States was not in existence today, I would not have the opportunity to excel in life and education. The Union was preserved, not only for the people yesterday, but also for the lives of today." Let us take inspiration from her words to continue the unfinished task so nobly advanced by those who gave the last full measure on this battlefield.

## Source

McPherson, James. Speech at Dedication Day Ceremony, Soldier's National Cemetery, Gettysburg, PA, November 19, 2000.

# IMPORTANT PEOPLE, PLACES, AND TERMS

**Abolitionists**
People who worked to end slavery.

**Beauregard, Pierre G. T. (1818-1893)**
Confederate general who captured Fort Sumter in April 1861.

**Buford, John (1826-1863)**
Union cavalry officer who played a leading role in enabling the Army of the Potomac to lay claim to strategically vital high ground at the Battle of Gettysburg.

**Census**
Official count of a nation's population.

**Chamberlain, Joshua Lawrence (1828-1914)**
Union officer best known for his leading role in the defense of Little Round Top at Gettysburg.

**Civil War**
Conflict that took place from 1861 to 1865 between Northern states (Union) and Southern seceded states (Confederacy); also known in the South as War Between the States.

**Confederacy**
Eleven Southern states that seceded from the United States in late 1860 and early 1861 and formed their own Confederate States of America (CSA).

**Davis, Jefferson (1808-1889)**
First and only president of the Confederate States of America (1861-1865).

**Early, Jubal A. (1816-1894)**
Confederate general who served in the Army of Northern Virginia at Gettysburg and many other battles; Early was also an early and prominent champion of the "Lost Cause" movement.

## Emancipation
The act of freeing people from slavery or oppression.

## Enlistment
The act of joining a state or country's military.

## Ewell, Richard S. (1817-1872)
Confederate corps commander in the Army of Northern Virginia at Gettysburg and several other battles.

## Federals
Soldiers of the U.S. army, better known as the Union army.

## Founding Fathers
Political leaders who founded the United States in 1776 and wrote the U.S. Constitution in 1787.

## Grant, Ulysses S. (1822-1885)
Union general who commanded Federal forces in several important victories, including battles at Vicksburg, Chattanooga, and Petersburg; Grant served as general-in-chief of all Union forces from March 1864 to the end of the war, and he later became the eighteenth president of the United States (1869-1877).

## Halleck, Henry W. (1815-1872)
General-in-chief of the Union army from July 1862-March 1864, after which he became Lincoln's chief of staff, March 1864-April 1865.

## Hancock, Winfield Scott (1824-1886)
Union general who became a war hero in the North for his command of Union defensive positions at the Battle of Gettysburg.

## Hill, "A. P." Ambrose Powell (1825-1865)
Confederate corps commander with the Army of Northern Virginia at Gettysburg and many other battles.

## Jackson, Thomas "Stonewall" (1824-1863)
Confederate lieutenant general who fought at First Bull Run, Second Bull Run, Antietam, Fredericksburg, and Chancellorsville; Jackson also led the 1862 Shenandoah Valley campaign.

**Johnston, Joseph E. (1807-1891)**
Confederate general of the Army of Tennessee; best known for his unsuccessful efforts to halt Sherman's capture of Atlanta and subsequent "March to the Sea."

**Lee, Robert E. (1807-1870)**
Confederate general who led the Army of Northern Virginia at Gettysburg, as well as at such other important battles as Second Bull Run, Antietam, Fredericksburg, Chancellorsville, and Petersburg.

**Lincoln, Abraham (1809-1865)**
Sixteenth president of the United States, 1861-1865.

**Longstreet, James (1821-1904)**
Confederate corps commander with the Army of Northern Virginia and a trusted advisor to General Robert E. Lee; repeatedly clashed with Lee over battle strategy at Gettysburg.

**Lost Cause**
A romanticized and often distorted account of the "Old South" and the Confederate war effort that describes white Southerners and their Civil War activities in a heroic light.

**March to the Sea**
The Union military campaign orchestrated by Union general William T. Sherman that swept across Georgia, from Atlanta to Savannah, from November 15 to December 21, 1864.

**McClellan, George (1826-1885)**
Union general who commanded the Army of the Potomac from August 1861 to November 1862; in 1864 McClellan became the Democratic nominee for president but lost to Lincoln in the November election.

**Meade, George G. (1815-1872)**
Union major general who commanded the Army of the Potomac from June 1863 to April 1865, including the Battle of Gettysburg of July 1-3, 1863.

**Pickett, George E. (1825-1875)**
Confederate general best known for leading "Pickett's Charge" on the decisive third day of the Battle of Gettysburg.

**Plantation**
A large Southern estate dedicated to farming.

**Rebel**
Confederate; often used as a term for Confederate soldiers.

**Secession**
Formal withdrawal of citizenship or membership from a country.

**Sectional**
Regional; usually used to refer to North-South differences in the years leading up to the Civil War.

**Sheridan, Philip (1831-1888)**
Union cavalry commander who led the Cavalry Corps of the Army of the Potomac in the Civil War's Eastern theatre in 1864-1865.

**Sherman, William Tecumseh (1820-1891)**
Union general who succeeded Grant as commander of Union forces in the Western theatre in 1864, and whose capture of Atlanta and subsequent "March to the Sea" played an important role in the Confederates' ultimate defeat.

**States' Rights**
The belief that each state has the right to decide how to handle various issues for itself without the influence or interference of the national government.

**Stuart, "Jeb" James Ewell Brown (1833-1864)**
Confederate cavalry officer with the Army of Northern Virginia whose extended absence during the Gettysburg campaign created planning problems for General Robert E. Lee.

**Underground Railroad**
Secret organization of free blacks and whites who helped slaves escape from their masters and gain freedom in the Northern United States and Canada.

**Union**
Northern states that remained loyal to the United States during the Civil War.

**Yankee**
Northerner; often used as a term for Union soldiers.

# CHRONOLOGY

**1775**

The Pennsylvania Abolition Society is founded in Philadelphia. *See p. 8.*

**1783**

The United States achieves independence from England. *See p. 8.*

**1787**

America's Founding Fathers establish the U.S. Constitution, a document expressing democratic principles and ideals that nonetheless largely avoids the issue of slavery. *See p. 8.*

**1793**

Eli Whitney invents the cotton gin, which deepens Southern dependence on cotton production—and, by extension, slave labor. *See p. 10.*

**1803**

A half-century of steady territorial expansion by the United States begins with the Louisiana Purchase, which transfers 828,000 square miles from French to American ownership. *See p. 12.*

**1820**

Congress passes the Missouri Compromise to regulate slavery in America's western territories. *See p. 12.*

**1850**

Congress passes the Compromise of 1850 in an effort to reduce sectional tensions over slavery, but provisions such as the Fugitive Slave Act further inflame hostilities between North and South. *See p. 15.*

**1852**

Harriet Beecher Stowe publishes the landmark anti-slavery novel *Uncle Tom's Cabin*. *See p. 17.*

**1854**

The Kansas-Nebraska Act is passed into law. *See p. 18.*

## 1857

The U.S. Supreme Court hands down its infamous *Dred Scott* decision, which stated that blacks could not be American citizens and opened the door to further expansion of slavery in the West. *See p. 20.*

## 1860

November 6 — Republican nominee Abraham Lincoln is elected president of the United States. *See p. 23.*

December 20 — South Carolina secedes from the United States. *See p. 25.*

## 1861

January 9-26 — Mississippi, Florida, Alabama, Georgia, and Louisiana secede from the Union. *See p. 25.*

February 1 — Texas lawmakers vote to secede from the Union. *See p. 25.*

February 18 — Jefferson Davis is inaugurated as the first provisional president of the Confederacy. *See p. 25.*

March 4 — Abraham Lincoln is sworn in as the sixteenth president of the United States. *See p. 26.*

April 12 — Confederate forces attack Fort Sumter in Charleston Harbor, South Carolina. *See p. 27.*

April 17 - June 8 — Virginia, Arkansas, Tennessee, and North Carolina secede from the United States. *See p. 27.*

May 20 — Kentucky claims neutrality in the Civil War. *See p. 27.*

July 21 — The first major battle of the Civil War, known as the First Battle of Bull Run or First Battle of Manassas, ends in a Confederate victory. *See p. 30.*

November 6 — Jefferson Davis is officially elected to a six-year term as president of the Confederate States of America.

## 1862

February 6, February 16 — Union victories at Fort Henry and Fort Donelson in Tennessee establish Ulysses S. Grant as one of the Federals' top generals. *See p. 33.*

March 17 — Union general George McClellan leads the Army of the Potomac on its Peninsular Campaign into Virginia. *See p. 35.*

April 6-7 — The Battle of Shiloh ends in a Union victory for General Ulysses S. Grant and his Army of the Tennessee. *See p. 34.*

April 25 — Union forces capture New Orleans *See p. 35.*

May 8 — Stonewall Jackson begins his successful Shenandoah Campaign in western Virginia. *See p. 36.*

June 25-July 1 — The Seven Days' Battles takes place between forces led by McClellan and Confederate general Robert E. Lee in eastern Virginia. *See p. 38.*

August 29-30 — Confederate forces win the Second Battle of Bull Run. *See p. 39.*

September 17 — The Battle of Antietam in Maryland ends in a bloody draw. *See p. 40.*

September 22 — President Lincoln announces the Emancipation Proclamation, which he signs on January 1, 1863. *See p. 41.*

December 13 — Confederate forces win the Battle of Fredericksburg. *See p. 42.*

## 1863

May 1-4 — Lee and the Army of Northern Virginia rout Union forces at the Battle of Chancellorsville. *See p. 54.*

June — West Virginia joins the Union as a slave state, agreeing to provisions that will gradually eliminate slavery in the state.

June 9 — The Battle of Brandy Station in Virginia between Union and Confederate cavalry ends in a standoff. *See p. 61.*

June 28 — Lincoln names General George G. Meade as the new commander of the Army of the Potomac. *See p. 63.*

July 1-3 — The Battle of Gettysburg erupts in southwestern Pennsylvania and ultimately ends in a devastating defeat for Lee and his Army of Northern Virginia. *See p. 65.*

July 4 — Confederate general John Pemberton surrenders Vicksburg, Mississippi, to Grant's Union forces after a long siege. *See p. 51.*

September 19-20 — Confederate forces win at the Battle of Chickamauga in Georgia. *See p. 100.*

November 19 — Lincoln delivers his famous Gettysburg Address. *See p. 101.*

November 23-25 — Union forces win the Battle of Chattanooga. *See p. 103.*

## 1864

March 10 — Grant is named general-in-chief of the entire Union army. *See p. 103.*

May-June — Grant and the Army of the Potomac repeatedly clash with Lee and the Army of Northern Virginia in a series of bloody skirmishes and battles. *See p. 103.*

June 15 — Grant begins a siege of Petersburg, a vital transportation artery for the Confederate capital of Richmond, Virginia. *See p. 104.*

August 5 — Union naval forces win the Battle of Mobile Bay. *See p. 104.*

September — Atlanta falls to Union forces led by General William T. Sherman. *See p. 104.*

September-October — Union forces under the command of General Philip Sheridan take control of the Shenandoah Valley, depriving Confederate armies of desperately needed supplies. *See p. 104.*

November 8 — Lincoln wins re-election, defeating Democratic nominee George McClellan. *See p. 104.*

November 15 — Sherman begins his March to the Sea after burning Atlanta. *See p. 105.*

December 21 — Sherman seizes Savannah, Georgia, and sends a telegraph to Lincoln offering the city as a Christmas present. *See p. 106.*

## 1865

March 4 — Lincoln is inaugurated for a second term.

April 2 — Petersburg falls to Grant's Union forces after a nine-month siege. *See p. 106.*

April 3 — Federal troops take over the Confederate capital of Richmond. *See p. 106.*

April 9 — Lee surrenders his Army of Northern Virginia to Grant at Appomattox Court House, Virginia. *See p. 108.*

April 14 — Lincoln is shot by John Wilkes Booth while attending a play in Washington, D.C. *See p. 111.*

April 15 — Lincoln dies and is succeeded by Andrew Johnson.

May 10 — Jefferson Davis is captured in Irwinville, Georgia.

April-May — Remaining Confederate armies surrender.

## 1865-1877

Federal economic and civil rights programs collectively known as Reconstruction are implemented across the South, only to be later dismantled by white Southerners who impose anti-black Jim Crow laws in their place. *See p. 112.*

## 1894

Congress establishes Gettysburg National Military Park. *See p. 114.*

## 1913

Gettysburg veterans hold a fiftieth anniversary gathering at the historic battlefield in Pennsylvania. *See p. 116.*

# SOURCES FOR
# FURTHER STUDY

*The Civil War: A Film by Ken Burns.* PBS, 1990. This famous nine-episode documentary series became one of the most popular programs ever broadcast over the Public Broadcasting System (PBS) when it was unveiled in 1990. The series, which blends archival photographs, live modern cinematography, music, narration, and interviews with historians to tell the story of the Civil War, is now available on DVD (the most recent "commemorative" version, released in 2011, includes previously unreleased interviews and commentary from director Ken Burns).

"Gettysburg," *Civil War Trust* website, n.d. Retrieved from http://www.civilwar.org/battlefields/gettysburg.html. This website contains a wide range of information on the Battle of Gettysburg, including high-quality maps, essays, historical articles, historical photographs, and links to other reputable Internet resources to learn more about the battle. The website was developed and is maintained by the Civil War Trust, a nonprofit organization devoted to the preservation of Civil War battlefields. Altogether, the Civil War Trust website (civilwar.org) provides summaries, maps, and other coverage of more than 100 Civil War battlefields.

Goodheart, Adam. "Civil War Battlefields: Saving the Landscape of America's Deadliest War." *National Geographic Magazine,* April 2005. Retrieved from http://ngm.nationalgeographic.com/ngm/0504/feature5/index.html. This *National Geographic* feature story utilizes the periodical's trademark blend of original writing and vivid photography to explain how many of America's historic Civil War battlefields have been endangered by commercial development.

Horwitz, Tony. *Confederates in the Attic: Dispatches from the Unfinished Civil War.* New York: Random House, 1998. A best-selling book that is equal parts travelogue and social history, *Confederates in the Attic* provides fascinating insights into the enduring passion that many Southerners continue to hold for the Civil War. During the course of his travels through the modern American South, Horwitz discusses the war and its continued importance to Southern culture with people ranging from Civil War re-enactors to Civil War historian Shelby Foote.

McPherson, James M. *Battle Cry of Freedom: The Civil War Era.* New York: Oxford University Press, 1988. This work ranks as one of the top one-volume histories of the Civil War.

Fast-paced, absorbing, and authoritative, *Battle Cry of Freedom* provides an interesting overview of the War Between the States and the events that led up to it.

The United States Civil War Center. Retrieved from http://www.cwc.lsu.edu/. This information clearinghouse maintained by Louisiana State University promotes the study of the Civil War with a wide range of features, including a Civil War cemetery database, a guide to researching people of the Civil War, a virtual history exhibit, reviews of books about the Civil War, and a "Blue and Gray for Boys and Girls" overview of young people's literature on the Civil War from the late nineteenth century to the present.

# BIBLIOGRAPHY

## Books

Boritt, Gabor. *The Gettysburg Gospel: The Lincoln Speech That Nobody Knows.* New York: Simon and Schuster, 2006.

Castel, Albert. *Decision in the West: The Atlanta Campaign of 1864.* Lawrence: University Press of Kansas, 1992.

Catton, Bruce. *The American Heritage New History of the Civil War.* New York: Viking, 1996.

Catton, Bruce. *This Hallowed Ground: A History of the Civil War.* 1955. Reprint. New York: Vintage, 2012.

Coddington, Edwin B. *The Gettysburg Campaign.* New York: Scribner's, 1968.

Desjardin, Thomas A. *These Honored Dead: How the Story of Gettysburg Shaped American Memory.* Cambridge, MA: Da Capo Press, 2003.

Foner, Eric. *The Fiery Trial: Abraham Lincoln and American Slavery.* New York: W. W. Norton, 2011.

Foote, Shelby. *The Civil War: A Narrative: Fort Sumter to Perryville.* New York: Random House, 1958.

Foote, Shelby. *The Civil War: A Narrative: Fredericksburg to Meridian.* New York: Random House, 1963.

Foote, Shelby. *The Civil War: A Narrative: Red River to Appomattox.* New York: Random House, 1974.

Gallagher, Gary W. *Lee and His Generals in War and Memory.* Baton Rouge: Louisiana State University Press, 2004.

Gallagher, Gary W., ed. *Two Witnesses at Gettysburg: The Personal Accounts of Whitelaw Reid and A. J. Fremantle.* Malden, MA: Wiley-Blackwell, 2009.

Hess, Earl J. *Pickett's Charge—The Last Attack at Gettysburg.* Chapel Hill: University of North Carolina Press, 2001.

Mansch, Larry D. *Abraham Lincoln, President-Elect: The Four Critical Months from Election to Inauguration.* Jefferson, NC: McFarland, 2005.

McClintock, Russell. *Lincoln and the Decision for War: The Northern Response to Secession.* Chapel Hill: University of North Carolina Press, 2008.

McPherson, James M. *Battle Cry of Freedom: The Civil War Era.* New York: Oxford University Press, 1988.

McPherson, James M. *Drawn with the Sword: Reflections on the American Civil War.* New York: Oxford University Press, 1996.

McPherson, James M. *Fields of Fury: The American Civil War.* New York: Atheneum, 2002.

McPherson, James M. *Hallowed Ground: A Walk at Gettysburg.* New York: Crown, 2003.

McPherson, James M. *Tried by War: Abraham Lincoln as Commander in Chief.* New York: Penguin Press, 2008.

Nofi, Albert A. *The Gettysburg Campaign: June-July 1863.* Revised edition. Conshohocken, PA: Combined Books, 1993.

Pfanz, Harry W. *Gettysburg: The Second Day.* Chapel Hill: University of North Carolina Press, 1987.

Reardon, Carol. *Pickett's Charge in History and Memory.* Chapel Hill: University of North Carolina Press, 1997.

Royster, Charles. *The Destructive War: William Tecumseh Sherman, Stonewall Jackson, and the Americans.* New York: HarperCollins, 1991.

Sandburg, Carl. *Abraham Lincoln: The War Years.* New York: Harcourt, Brace and Company, 1939.

Sears, Stephen W. *Gettysburg.* Boston: Houghton Mifflin, 2003.

Time-Life Editors. *Gettysburg: The Confederate High Tide (The Civil War Series).* Alexandria, VA: Time-Life Books, 1985.

Trudeau, Noah Andre. *Gettysburg: A Testing of Courage.* New York: HarperCollins, 2002.

Trudeau, Noah Andre. *Southern Storm: Sherman's March to the Sea.* New York: HarperCollins, 2008.

Ward, Geoffrey, with Ric Burns and Ken Burns. *The Civil War.* New York: Vintage Books, 1994.

## Online Resources

*African American Civil War Memorial & Museum.* n.d. Retrieved from http://www.afroamcivilwar.org/.

*The Civil War: A Film by Ken Burns* [online]. PBS, 1990. Retrieved from http://www.pbs.org/civilwar/.

*Civil War Animated.* n.d. Retrieved from http://civilwaranimated.com/.

Wert, Jeffry. "America's Civil War: Robert E. Lee and James Longstreet at Odds at Gettysburg." *Military History,* August 1994. Retrieved from http://www.historynet.com/americas -civil-war-robert-e-lee-and-james-longstreet-at-odds-at-gettysburg.htm.

## DVD/Blu-Ray

*The Civil War: A Film by Ken Burns.* PBS, 1990.

*Robert E. Lee: At War with His Country … and Himself* (American Experience). PBS, 2011.

# PHOTO AND ILLUSTRATION CREDITS

Cover and Title Page: *Capt. Howard and group. Office of Assistant Quartermaster, Army of Potomac. Fairfax Court House, June 1863 Gettysburg Campaign.* Photograph by Timothy H. O'Sullivan, Civil War Glass Negative Collection, Prints & Photographs Division, Library of Congress, LC-B817-7549.

Chapter One: Photograph of a painting by Howard Chandler Christy on display in the U.S. Capitol, Prints & Photographs Division, Library of Congress, LC-USA7-34630 (p. 9); Courtesy National Archives, photo no. 165-JT-230 (p. 11); Prints & Photographs Division, Library of Congress, LC-DIG-ppmsca-15708 (p. 12); Prints & Photographs Division, Library of Congress, LC-DIG-ppmsca-19251 (p. 14); Lithograph by N. Currier, Prints & Photographs Division, Library of Congress, LC-DIG-ppmsca-00774 (p. 16); Prints & Photographs Division, Library of Congress, LC-DIG-ppmsca-11212 (p. 18); Photograph by Black & Batchelder, Prints & Photographs Division, Library of Congress, LC-DIG-ppmsca-23763 (p. 19); © North Wind Picture Archives/The Image Works (p. 21); Lithograph by W. H. Rease (Philadelphia, c.1860), Prints & Photographs Division, Library of Congress, LC-USZC4-7996 (p. 22).

Chapter Two: Brady-Handy Collection, Prints & Photographs Division, Library of Congress, LC-DIG-cwpbh-00879 (p. 26); Illustrated in Harper's Weekly (1861 April 27), Prints & Photographs Division, Library of Congress, LC-USZ62-90258 (p. 28); From Frank Leslie's Illustrated Newspaper (1864 March 19), Prints & Photographs Division, Library of Congress, LC-USZ62-93555 (p. 29); Calabria Design/Copyright © 2012 Omnigraphics, Inc. (p. 31); Prints & Photographs Division, Library of Congress, LC-DIG-pga-00335 (p. 33); Photograph by Frederick Gutekunst, Prints & Photographs Division, Library of Congress, LC-USZ62-1770 (p. 34); Lithograph by Thomas S. Sinclair, Prints & Photographs Division, Library of Congress, LC-USZ62-15627 (p. 36); Lithograph by J. H. Bufford, Prints & Photographs Division, Library of Congress, LC-DIG-pga-00378 (p. 37); Photograph by Julian Vannerson, Civil War Glass Negatives and Related Prints Collection, Prints & Photographs Division, Library of Congress, LC-DIG-cwpb-04402 (p. 38); Civil War Photograph Collection, Prints & Photographs Division, Library of Congress, LC-DIG-stereo-1s02860 (p. 39); Photograph by Alexander Gardner, Civil War Glass Negatives and Related Prints Collection, Prints & Photographs Division, Library of Congress, LC-DIG-cwpb-01097 (p. 41); Print by Allen

Christian Redwood, Prints & Photographs Division, Library of Congress, LC-USZ62-134479 (p. 43).

Chapter Three: Lithograph by Kurz & Allison, Prints & Photographs Division, Library of Congress, LC-DIG-pga-01858 (p. 48); Print by Prang (L.) & Co., Prints & Photographs Division, Library of Congress, LC-DIG-pga-04049 (p. 52); Civil War Glass Negatives and Related Prints Collection, Prints & Photographs Division, Library of Congress, LC-USZ62-111519 (p. 54); Currier & Ives, Prints & Photographs Division, Library of Congress, LC-cph-3b35218 (p. 55); Prints & Photographs Division, Library of Congress, LC-USZ62-51832 (p. 57); Calabria Design/Copyright © 2012 Omnigraphics, Inc. (p. 59); Drawing by Edwin Forbes, Morgan Collection of Civil War Drawings, Prints & Photographs Division, Library of Congress, LC-DIG-ppmsca-22378 (p. 61); Civil War Glass Negatives and Related Prints Collection, Prints & Photographs Division, Library of Congress, LC-DIG-cwpb-07542 (p. 63).

Chapter Four: Civil War Glass Negatives and Related Prints Collection, Prints & Photographs Division, Library of Congress, LC-cwpb-06372 (p. 67); Original mezzotint by Max Rosenthal (1897), Prints & Photographs Division, Library of Congress, LC-USZ62-114303 (p. 69); Civil War Glass Negatives and Related Prints Collection, Prints & Photographs Division, Library of Congress, LC-USZ62-52492 (p. 71); Calabria Design/Copyright © 2012 Omnigraphics, Inc. (p. 73); Civil War Collection, Prints & Photographs Division, Library of Congress, LC-USZ62-55424 (p. 75); Prints & Photographs Division, Library of Congress, LC-DIG-pga-03235 (p. 76); Calabria Design/Copyright © 2012 Omnigraphics, Inc. (p. 77); Prints & Photographs Division, Library of Congress, LC-USZ62-100659 (p. 79); © North Wind Picture Archives/The Image Works (p. 80); Civil War Glass Negatives and Related Prints Collection, Prints & Photographs Division, Library of Congress, LC-cwpb-05828 (p. 82); Civil War Glass Negatives and Related Prints Collection, Prints & Photographs Division, Library of Congress, LC-DIG-cwpb-03981 (p. 83).

Chapter Five: Calabria Design/Copyright © 2012 Omnigraphics, Inc. (p. 87); © Mary Evans Picture Library/The Image Works (p. 89); Civil War Glass Negatives and Related Prints Collection, Prints & Photographs Division, Library of Congress, LC-DIG-cwpb-07523 (p. 91); The Granger Collection, New York (p. 92); Photograph by Alexander Gardner, Civil War Glass Negatives and Related Prints Collection, Prints & Photographs Division, Library of Congress, LC-DIG-cwpb-00882 (p. 94); Photograph by Mathew B. Brady, Prints & Photographs Division, Library of Congress, LC-DIG-ppmsca-19211 (p. 96).

Chapter Six: Prints & Photographs Division, Library of Congress, LC-USZ61-903 (p. 100); Prints & Photographs Division, Library of Congress, LC-DIG-ppmsca-19926 (p. 102); Civil War Collection, Prints & Photographs Division, Library of Congress, LC-DIG-ppmsca-23730 (p. 105); Civil War Glass Negatives and Related Prints Collection, Prints & Photographs Division, Library of Congress, LC-DIG-cwpb-07136 (p. 106); Civil War Glass Negatives and Related Prints Collection, Prints & Photographs Division, Library of Congress, LC-DIG-cwpb-02709 (p. 107); Prints & Photographs Division, Library of Congress, LC-DIG-pga-02091 (p. 108).

Chapter Seven: Highsmith (Carol M.) Archive, Prints & Photographs Division, Library of Congress, LC-DIG-highsm-13020 (p. 115); Civil War, Prints & Photographs Division, Library of Congress, LC-USZ62-88416 (p. 116); Hoxie Collection, Prints & Photographs Division, Library of Congress, LC-USZ61-2064 (p. 119); Highsmith (Carol M.) Archive, Prints & Photographs Division, Library of Congress, LC-DIG-highsm-12542 (p. 120).

Biographies: Civil War Glass Negatives and Related Prints Collection, Prints & Photographs Division, Library of Congress, LC-cwpbh-03163 (p. 125); Prints & Photographs Division, Library of Congress, LC-USZ62-101468 (p. 129); Civil War Glass Negatives and Related Prints Collection, Prints & Photographs Division, Library of Congress, LC-USZ62-131810 (p. 134); Civil War Glass Negatives and Related Prints Collection, Prints & Photographs Division, Library of Congress, LC-DIG-cwpbh-03116 (p. 138); Photograph by Alexander Gardner, Prints & Photographs Division, Library of Congress, LC-cph-3a53289 (p. 143); Civil War Glass Negatives and Related Prints Collection, Prints & Photographs Division, Library of Congress, LC-DIG-cwpb-06085 (p. 148); Civil War Glass Negatives and Related Prints Collection, Prints & Photographs Division, Library of Congress, LC-DIG-cwpb-05008 (p. 153); Brady-Handy Collection, Prints & Photographs Division, Library of Congress, LC-DIG-cwpbh-00682 (p. 157); Civil War Glass Negatives and Related Prints Collection, Prints & Photographs Division, Library of Congress, LC-DIG-cwpb-07546 (p. 161).

# INDEX